The Art of Poetry, volume 19

Cambridge IGCSE, *Songs of Ourselves*

PERIPETEIA PRESS

Published by Peripeteia Press Ltd.

First published August 2019

ISBN: 978-1-999737665

Check out our A-level English Literature website, peripeteia.webs.com

Contents

General Introduction to The Art of Poetry

The philosopher Nietzsche described his work as 'the greatest gift that [mankind] has ever been given'. The Elizabethan poet Edmund Spenser hoped his epic, *The Faerie Queene*, would magically transform its readers into noblemen. In comparison, our aims for *The Art of Poetry* series of books are a little more modest. Fundamentally we aim to provide books that will be of maximum use to English students and their teachers. In our experience, few students read essays on poems, yet, whatever specification they are studying, they have to write analytical essays on poetry. So, we're offering some models, written in a lively, accessible and, we hope, engaging style. We believe that the essay as a form needs demonstrating and championing, especially as so many revision books for students present information in broken down note form.

For Volume 1 we chose canonical poems for several reasons: Firstly, they are simply great poems, well worth reading and studying; secondly, we chose poems from across time so that they sketch in outline major developments in English poetry, from the Elizabethan period up until the present day, so that the volume works as an introduction to poetry and poetry criticism. Our popular volumes 2-5 focused on poems set at A-level by the Edexcel and AQA boards respectively. Volumes 6 to 11 tackled GCSE anthologies from AQA, Eduqas, OCR and Edexcel's. In this current volume, we our focus turns to IGCSE, providing critical support for students reading poems about from Cambridge's IGCSE poetry anthology. In particular, we hope our book will inspire those students aiming to reach the very highest grades.

Introduction to Volume 19, *Songs of Ourselves*

Like every other GCSE examination board, CIE are looking for perceptive reading, sophisticated understanding and precise analysis of language and of poetic devices. In examiners' speak you have to demonstrate 'critical understanding', 'respond sensitively and in detail to the way the writer achieves his/her effects' and you have to 'integrate much well-selected reference to the text' into your answer. For the highest grade, A* in old money, 9 in the new numerical grading system, you also have to do all this, like Heidi and her blue hair, i.e. with a touch of 'individuality and flair'. One way of learning how to demonstrate that individuality and flair is to follow the advice set out in this book. We put a premium on responses to the poems that do not follow a pre-set agenda or essay recipe and we think your writing should express your own thoughts and feelings informed by your teachers, your peers and your wider reading. And we believe your critical understanding should be expressed in your own emerging critical voice. Hopefully reading our essays will also help too. But to hit the very top, you'll need to supplement what we have written in our essays with your own observations about the poems. The whole of your essay doesn't need to be original and you don't need to completely reinvent the essay form, but a little originality goes a long way, in life, in art and in Literature exams.

Unlike other examination boards, CIE puts a premium on your own response to the poems. Their list of adjectives describing top level performance is: 'perceptive, convincing and relevant'. The last of these doesn't sound too demanding, except that it qualifies 'personal' - a 'relevant, personal response'. Now, ideally what CIE are after is what we have just described - an essay that conveys your own thoughts, informed by others, expressed in your own critical voice. What they absolutely do not want is the mere repetition of a model essay that has been provided by a secondary source, whether this source is a teacher, the internet or even a book like this. Nor do they want from a school's GCSE cohort identikit essays all following exactly the same structure, all using the same evidence with the same analysis, all expressing the same ideas and second-hand opinions with varying degrees of confidence.

When you are developing knowledge and understanding of these poems and of how to write successful Literature essays it can be very helpful to use writing frames. And, of course, it is also fine if the bulk of your essay communicates the analysis you, your class and/or your  teacher have developed on the poems, or, indeed you pick up from reading our essays. But like a child learning to ride a bike, if you want to reach the top grades, at some point you need to dispense with the stabilisers and go it alone. If your teacher always insists you follow a writing framework, try to provide original analysis within this. Or, if you're feeling bolder, delight your teacher by breaking out of the frame and producing something more individual and original. Just make sure that the content is very good and that the frame is robust.

If you develop your own appreciation, if you write essays that genuinely express your own, informed thinking and you do this well, you will reach a top grade. In an ideal world everyone in your class would produce different responses, because we are all different and have different tastes, preferences, life experiences and so forth. However, it's also helpful to be realistic about this and to have a few tricks up your sleeve, just to make sure the CIE examiners credit you fully for the personal element of your response. It's worth bearing in mind that automatically you will not reach A*, or 9, unless there is clear evidence of this personal dimension to your essay. And also remember that it is only on the poetry essay that you have to demonstrate this.

—

So, our advice is that in your poetry essay you draw explicit attention to yourself as a reader at least a few times, perhaps three times over the course of your essay. Generally using the first person singular 'I' is considered naive style in academic literary essays, so we recommend instead you use the phrases 'for me' and 'in my opinion'. Clearly there's little point in employing these phrases before factual information. Writing 'for me Morris' poem is called *Little Boy Crying*' would be stupid, obviously. Reserve these phrases for when you are evaluating the effectiveness of a device or feature, as in, 'for me the most powerful way in which Mew expresses her distress is through the form of her poem'. Now that is an opinion, one that you're going to have to use evidence, and use it well, to persuade someone else to accept. These personalising phrases can also usefully be employed in your conclusion to provide a final, distinctively individual angle on the poem and the essay title.

The examination

In the Literature exam. you will have to write one poetry essay. You will be given a choice of two questions on the poems from the *Songs of Ourselves* poetry anthology. Both questions will name specific poems and will include a printed copy of them. Mostly CIE exam questions ask you to respond to one specific poem and they tend to phrase their questions in the 'how does the writer' style. This should focus your attention on the key aspects of what the writer has to say about the topic of the poem and what methods they use to explore this topic. Occasionally, CIE set a question with two short poems. It's important to know that in the exam, if you choose to write on two poems that there are no marks set aside for comparison. You can, in fact, write about the poems separately and still achieve full marks. Hence, this seems to be a more difficult task and we'd generally recommend that you don't choose it.

In their examination reports CIE often comment on the fact that many pupils ignore the little, but essential, word 'how' which should focus your attention on writers' methods. And here are a few more useful words of wisdom from the chief examiner's report:

'The key distinguishing factor [between levels of response] was the extent to which candidates were able to assess the impact of their chosen lines. Some simply repeated the word "powerful" from the question, without really thinking about why [they found] the lines so powerful.'

An adventure into what one apprehends

When writing about themes, students often simply state what they think the major theme of a poem to be. Clearly writing 'this poem is about family relationships' is a reasonable start, but it's a start that needs careful development. Sometimes readers also labour under misconceptions about the nature of poetry, believing, for example, that poems have secret meanings which, rather annoyingly, poets have hidden under deliberately obscure language. The task of the reader becomes to decode the obscure verbiage and extract the secreted message. Unsurprisingly, this misconception of poetry as a sort of self-regarding subcategory of fables makes readers wonder why poets go to all the irritating trouble of hiding their messages in the first place. If they had something to say, why didn't the poet just say it straightforwardly and save everyone - teachers, students, examiners - a lot of unnecessary fuss and bother? Why couldn't Rich, for instance, have just said that women try to heal earth's wounds?

The Romantic poet, John Keats' comment about distrusting poetry that has a 'palpable design' on the reader has been much quoted. For Keats, and many poets, a 'palpable design' is an aspect of rhetoric and particularly of propaganda. And a poem is not just a piece of propaganda for a poet's ideas. As the modern poet, George Szirtes puts it, poems are not 'rhymed advertisements for the already formed views of poets'. Here's George discussing the issue in his blog [ttp://georgeszirtes.blogspot.co.uk/]:

'A proper poem has to be a surprise: no surprise for the poet no surprise for the reader, said Robert Frost and I think that he and Keats were essentially right. A proper poem should arise out of a naked unguarded experience that elicits surprise in the imagination by extending the consciousness in some way. Poetry is not what one knows but an adventure into what one apprehends.'

Most poems, and all really good ones, are not merely prettified presentations of a poet's settled views about a particular theme or issue; they are more like thought experiments or journeys of exploration and discovery, as they are for us as readers. In other words, poetry, like all art, is equipment for thinking and feeling. So, instead of writing that 'poem x is about death' try to think more carefully through what is interesting or unusual or surprising about the poem's exploration of these subjects. Approach a poem with questions in mind: What does the poem have to say about its theme? What angle does the poet take; is the poem celebratory, mournful, exploratory? To what extent does the poem take up arms and argue for something and have a 'palpable design'? Is the attitude to the subject consistent or does it change? To what extent is the poem philosophical or emotional? Do we learn something new, does it change how we think or feel? How might the poem have extended our thinking about its subject? Then you can relate any techniques you identify in the poet back to these overarching questions.

An adventure into what you apprehend is a great way to conceptualise a poem. And it's very productive too as a way to think about writing poetry criticism, to which theme we turn next.

How to analyse a poem [seen or unseen]

A list of ingredients, not a recipe

Firstly, what not to do: sometimes pupils have been so programmed to spot poetic features such as alliteration that they start analysis of a poem with close reading of these micro aspects of technique. This is never a good idea. A far better strategy is to begin by trying to develop an overall understanding of what you think the poem is about. While, obviously, all these poems are about relationships of some sort or other, the nature of these relationships vary widely and what they have say about this topic is also highly varied. Once you've established the central concerns, you can delve into the poem's interior, examining its inner workings in the light of these. And you should be flexible enough to adapt, refine or even reject your initial thoughts in the light of your investigation. The essential thing is to make sure that whether you're discussing imagery or stanza form, sonic effects or syntax, enjambment or vocabulary, you always explore the significance of the feature in terms of meanings and effect.

Someone once compared texts to cakes. When you're presented with a cake the first thing you notice is what it looks like. Probably the next thing you'll do is taste it and find out if you like the flavour. This aesthetic experience will come first. Only later might you investigate the ingredients and how it was made. Adopting a uniform reading strategy is like a recipe; it sets out what you must do, step by step, in a predetermined order. This can be helpful, especially when you start reading and analysing poems. Hence in our first volume in *The Art of Poetry* series we explored each poem under the same subheadings of narrator, characters, imagery, patterns of sound, form & structure and contexts, and all our essays followed essentially the same direction. Of course, this is a reasonable strategy for reading poetry and will stand you in good stead. However, this present volume takes a different, more flexible approach, because this book is designed for students aiming for levels 7 to 9, or A to A* in old currency, and to reach the highest levels your work needs to be a bit more conceptual, critical and individual. Writing frames are useful for beginners, like stabilisers when you learn to ride a bike. But, if you wish to write top level essays you need to develop your own frames.

Read our essays and you'll find that they all include the same principle ingredients – detailed, 'fine-grained' reading of crucial elements of poetry, imagery, form, rhyme and so forth - but each essay starts in a different way and each one has a slightly different focus or weight of attention on the various aspects that make up a poem. Once you feel you have mastered the apprentice strategy of reading all poems in the same way, we strongly recommend you put this generic essay recipe approach to one side and move on to a new way of reading, an approach that can change depending on the nature of the poem you're reading.

Follow your nose
Having established what you think a poem is about - its theme and what is interesting about the poet's treatment of the theme [the conceptual bit] - rather than then working through a pre-set agenda, decide what you honestly think are the most interesting aspects of the poem and start analysing these closely. This way your response will be original [a key marker of a top band essay] and you'll be writing about material you find most interesting. In other words, you're foregrounding yourself as an individual, critical reader. These most interesting aspects might be ideas or technique based, or both.

Follow your own, informed instincts, trust in your own critical intelligence as a reader. If you're writing about material that genuinely interests you, your writing is likely to be interesting for the examiner too. And, obviously, take advice to from your teacher too, use their expertise.

Because of the focus on sonic effects and imagery other aspects of poems are often overlooked by students. It is a rare student, for instance, who notices how punctuation works in a poem and who can write about it convincingly. Few students write about the contribution of the unshowy function words, such as pronouns, prepositions or conjunctions, yet these words are crucial to any text. Of course, it would be a highly risky strategy to focus your whole essay on a seemingly innocuous and incidental detail of a poem. But coming at things from an unusual angle is as important to writing great essays as it is to the production of great poetry.

So, in summary, when reading a poem for the first time, such as when doing an 'unseen' style question, have a check list in mind, but don't feel you must follow someone else's generic essay recipe. Don't feel that you must always start with a consideration of imagery if the poem you're analysing has, for instance, an eye-catching form. Consider the significance of major features, such as imagery, vocabulary, sonic patterns and form. Try to write about these aspects in terms of their contribution to themes and effects. But also follow your nose, find your own direction, seek out aspects that genuinely engage you and write about these.

The essays in this volume provide examples and we hope they will encourage you to go your own way, at least to some extent, and to make discoveries for yourself. No single essay could possibly cover everything that could be said about any one of these poems; aiming to create comprehensive essays like this would be utterly foolish. And we have not tried to do so. Nor are our essays meant to be models for exam essays – they're far too long for that. They do, however, illustrate the sort of conceptualised, critical and 'fine-grained' exploration demanded for top grades at GCSE and beyond. There's always more to be discovered, more to say, space in other words for you to develop some original reading of your own, space for you to write your own individual essay recipe.

Writing Literature essays

The **Big** picture and the small

An essay itself can be a form of art. And writing a great essay takes time, skill and practice. And also expert advice. Study the two figures in the picture carefully and describe what you can see. Channel your inner Sherlock Holmes to add any deductions you are able to form about the image. Before reading what we have to say, write your description out as a prose paragraph. Probably you'll have written something along the following lines:

First off, the overall impression: this picture is very blurry. Probably this indicates that either this is a very poor-quality reproduction, or that it is a copy of a very small detail from a much bigger image that has been magnified several times. The image shows a stocky man and a medium-sized dog, both orientated towards something to their left, which suggests there is some point of interest in that direction. From the man's rustic dress (smock, breeches, clog-like boots) the picture is either an old one or a modern one depicting the past. The man appears to be carrying a stick and there's maybe a bag on his back. From all of these details we can probably deduce that he's a peasant, maybe a farmer or a shepherd.

Now do the same thing for picture two. We have even less detail here and again the picture's blurry. Particularly without the benefit of colour it's hard to determine what we're seeing other than a horizon and maybe the sky. We might just be able to make out that in the centre of the picture is the shape of the sun. From the reflection, we can deduce that the image is of the sun, either setting or rising over water. If it is dawn this usually symbolises hope, birth and new beginnings; if the sun is setting it conventionally symbolises the opposite – the end of things, the coming of night/ darkness, death.

If you're a sophisticated reader, you might well start to think about links between the two images. Are they, perhaps, both details from the same single larger image, for instance.

Well, this image might be even harder to work out. Now we don't even

 have a whole figure, just a leg, maybe, sticking up in the air. Whatever is happening here, it looks painful and we can't even see the top half of the body. From the upside orientation, we might guess that the figure is or has fallen. If we put this image with the one above, we might think the figure has fallen into water as there are

horizontal marks on the image that could be splashes. From the quality of this image we can deduce that this is an even smaller detail blown-up.

You may be wondering by now why we've suddenly moved into rudimentary art appreciation. On the other hand, you may already have worked out the point of this exercise. Either way, bear with us, because this is the last picture for you to describe and analyse. So, what have we here? Looks like another peasant, again from the past, perhaps medieval (?) from the smock-like dress, clog-like shoes and the britches. This character is also probably male and seems to be pushing some wooden apparatus from left to right. From the ridges at the bottom left of the image we can surmise that he's working the land,  probably pushing a plough. Noticeably, the figure has his back to us;

we see he has turned away from us, suggesting he is wholly concentrated on the task at hand. In the background appear to be sheep, which would fit with our impression that this is an image of farming. It seems likely that this image and the first one come from the same painting. They have a similar style and subject and it is possible that these sheep belong to our first character. This image is far less blurry than the other one. Either it is a better-quality reproduction, or this is a larger, more significant detail extracted from the original source. If this is a significant detail, it's interesting that we cannot see the character's face. From this we can deduce that he's not important in and of himself; rather he's a representative figure and the important thing is what he is and what he isn't looking at.

Okay, we hope we haven't stretched your patience too far. What's the point of all this? Well, let's imagine we prefixed the paragraphs above with an introduction, along the following lines: 'The painter makes this picture interesting and powerful by using several key techniques and details' and that we added a conclusion, along the lines of 'So now I have shown how the painter has made this picture interesting and powerful through the use of a number of key techniques and details'. Finally, substitute painter and picture for writer and text. If we put together our paragraphs into an essay what would be its strengths and weaknesses? What might be a better way of writing our essay?

Consider the strengths first off. The best bits of our essay, we humbly suggest, are the bits where we begin to explain what we are seeing, when we do the Holmes-like deductive thinking. Another strength might be that we have started to make links between the various images, or parts of a larger image, to see how they work together to provide us more information. A corresponding weakness is that each of our paragraphs seems like a separate chunk of writing. The weaker parts of the paragraphs are where we simply describe what we can see. More importantly though, if we used our comments on image one as our first paragraph we seem to have started in a rather random way. Why should we have begun our essay with that image? What was the logic behind that? And most importantly of all, if this image is an analogue for a specific aspect of a text, such as a poem's imagery or a novel's dialogue we have dived straight into to analysing this technical aspect before we're established any overall sense of the painting/ text. And this is a very common fault with GCSE English Literature essays. As we've said before and will keep saying, pupils start writing detailed micro-analysis of a detail such as alliteration before they have established the big picture of what the text is about and what the answer to the question they've been set might be. Without this big picture it's very difficult to write about the significance of the micro details. And the major marks for English essays are reserved for explanations of the significance and effects generated by a writer's craft.

Now we'll try a different and much better approach. Let's start off with the big picture, the whole image. The painting below is called *Landscape with the fall of Icarus*. It's usually attributed to the Renaissance artist, Pieter Breughel and was probably painted in the 1560s. Icarus is a character from Greek mythology. He was the son of the brilliant inventor, Daedalus. Trapped on Crete by the evil King Minos, Daedalus and Icarus managed to escape when the inventor created pairs of giant feathered wings. Before they took to sky Daedalus warned his son not

to get too excited and fly too near the sun as the wings were held together by wax that might melt. Icarus didn't listen, however. The eventual result was that he plummeted back to earth, into the sea more precisely and was killed.

Applying this contextual knowledge to the painting we can see that the image is about how marginal Icarus' tragedy is in the big picture. Conventionally we'd expect any image depicting such a famous myth to make Icarus's fall the dramatic centre of attention. The main objects of this painting, however, are emphatically not the falling boy hitting the water. Instead our eye is drawn to the peasant in the centre of the painting, pushing his plough [even more so in colour as his shirt is the only red object in an otherwise greeny-yellow landscape] and the stately galleon sailing calmly past those protruding legs. Seeing the whole image, we can appreciate the significance of the shepherd and the ploughman looking up and down and to the left. The point being made is how they don't even notice the tragedy because they have work to do and need to get on with their lives. The animals too seem unconcerned. As W. H. Auden puts it, in lines from *Musée des Beaux Arts*, 'everything turns away / Quite leisurely from the disaster'.

To sum up, when writing an essay on any literary text do not begin with close-up analysis of micro-details. Begin instead with establishing the whole picture: What the text is about, what key techniques the writer uses, when it was written, what sort of text it is, what effects it has on the reader. Then, when you zoom in to examine smaller details, such as imagery, individual words, metre or sonic techniques you can discuss these in relation to their significance in terms of this bigger picture.

What would our art appreciation essay look like now?

Paragraph #1: Introduction – myth of Icarus, date of painting, the way our eyes are drawn away from his tragic death to much more ordinary life going around him. Significance of this – even tragic suffering goes on around us without us even noticing, we're too busy getting on with our lives.

Paragraph #2: We could, of course, start with our first figure and follow the same order as we've presented the images here. But wouldn't it make more logical sense to discuss first the biggest, more prominent images in the painting first? So, our first paragraph is about the ploughman and his horse. How his figure is placed centrally and is bent downwards towards the ground and turned left away from us etc.

Paragraph #3: The next most prominent image is the ship. Also moving from right to left, as if the main point of interest in the painting is off in that direction. Here we could consider the other human agricultural figure, the shepherd and his dog and, of course, the equally oblivious sheep.

Paragraph #4: Having moved on to examining background details in the painting we could discuss the symbolism of the sun on the horizon. While this could be the sun rising, the context of the story suggests it is more likely to be setting. The pun of the sun/son going down makes sense.

Paragraph #5: Finally, we can turn our attention to the major historical and literary figure in this painting, Icarus and how he is presented. This is the key image in terms of understanding the painting's purpose and effect.

Paragraph #6: Conclusion. What is surprising about this picture. How do the choices the painter makes affect us as viewer/ reader? Does this painting make Icarus's story seem more pathetic, more tragic or something else?

Now, all you have to do is switch from a painting to a poem.

Big pictures, big cakes, recipes and lists of instructions; following your own nose and going your own way. Whatever metaphors we use, your task is to bring something personal and individual to your critical reading of poems and to your essay writing.

Writing about language

Poems are paintings as well as windows; we look at them as well as through them. As you know, special attention should be paid to language in poetry because of all the literary art forms poetry, in particular, employs language in a precise, self-conscious and distinctive way. Ideally in poetry, every word should count. Analysis of language falls into distinct categories:

- By diction we mean the vocabulary used in a poem. A poem might be composed from the ordinary language of everyday speech or it might use elaborate, technical or elevated phrasing. Or both. At one time, some words and types of words were considered inappropriate for the rarefied field of poetry. The great Irish poet, W. B. Yeats never referred to modern technology in his poetry, there are no cars, or tractors or telephones, because he did not consider such things fitting for poetry. When much later, Philip Larkin used swear words in his otherwise well-mannered verse the effect was deeply shocking. Modern poets have pretty much dispensed with the idea of there being an elevated literary language appropriate for poetry. Hence in the CIE anthology you'll find all sorts of modern, everyday language.

- Grammatically a poem may use complex or simple sentences [the key to which is the conjunctions]; it might employ a wash of adjectives and adverbs, or it may rely extensively on the bare force of nouns and verbs. Picking out and exploring words from specific grammatical classes has the merit of being both incisive and usually illuminating.

- Poets might mix together different types, conventions and registers of language, moving, for example, between formal and informal, spoken and written, modern and archaic, and so forth. Arranging the diction in the poem in terms of lexico-semantic fields, by register or by etymology, helps reveal underlying patterns of meaning.

- For almost all poems imagery is a crucial aspect of language. Broadly imagery is a synonym for description and can be broken down into two types, sensory and figurative. Sensory imagery means the words and phrases that appeal to our senses, to touch and taste, hearing, smell and sight. Sensory imagery is evocative; it helps to take us into the world of the poem to share the experience being described. Figurative imagery, in particular, is always significant. As we have mentioned, not all poems rely on metaphors and similes; these devices are only part of a poet's box of tricks, but figurative language is always important when it occurs because it compresses multiple meanings into itself. To use a technical term figurative images are polysemic - they contain many meanings. Try writing out the all the meanings contained in a metaphor in a more concise and economical way. Even simple, everyday metaphors compress meaning. If we want to say our teacher is fierce and powerful and that we fear his or her wrath, we can more concisely say our teacher is a dragon.

Writing about patterns of sound

Like painters, some poets have powerful visual imaginations, while other poets have stronger auditory imaginations and are more like musicians. Hence, while some poems are like paintings, others are more like pieces of music.

Firstly, what not to do: Tempting as it may be to spot sonic features of a poem and list these, don't do this. Avoid something along the lines of 'The poet uses alliteration here and the rhyme scheme is ABABCDCDEFEFGG'. Sometimes, indeed, it may be tempting to set out the poem's whole rhyme scheme like this. Resist the temptation: This sort of identification of features is worth zero marks. Marks in exams are reserved for attempts to link techniques to meanings and to effects.

Probably many of us have been sitting in English lessons listening somewhat sceptically as our English teacher explains the surprisingly specific significance of a seemingly random piece of alliteration in a poem. Something along the lines 'The double d sounds here reinforce a sense of invincible strength' or 'the harsh repetition of the 't' sounds suggests anger'. Through all our minds at some point may have passed the idea that, in these instances, English teachers appear to be using some sort of Enigma-style secret symbolic decoding machine that reveals how particular patterns of sounds have such definite encoded meanings.

And this sort of thing is not all nonsense. Originally deriving from an oral tradition, poems are, of course, written for the ear as much as for the eye, to be heard as much as read. A poem is a soundscape as much as it is a set of meanings. Sounds are, however, difficult to tie to very definite meanings and effects. By way of example, the old BBC Radiophonic workshop, which produced ambient sounds for radio andtelevision programmes, used the same sounds in different contexts, knowing that the audience would perceive them in the appropriate way because of that context. Hence the sound of bacon sizzling of an audience clapping and of feet walking over gravel were actually recordings of an identical sound. Listeners heard them differently because of the context. So, we may, indeed, be able to spot the repeated 's' sounds in a poem, but whether this creates a hissing sound, yes like a snake, or the susurration of the sea will depend on the context within

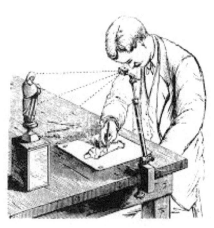

the poem and the ears of the reader. Whether a sound is soft and soothing or harsh and grating is also open to interpretation.

The idea of connecting these sounds to meanings or significance is a productive one. And your analysis will be most convincing if you use several pieces of evidence together. In other words, rather than try to pick out individual examples of sonic effects we recommend you explore the weave or pattern of sounds, the effects these generate and their contribution to feelings and ideas. For example, this might mean examining how alliteration and assonance are used together to achieve a particular mimetic effect.

Writing about form & structure

As you know, there are no marks for simply identifying textual features. This holds true for language, sounds and also for form. Consider instead the relationship between a poem's form and its content, themes and effects. Form is not merely decorative or ornamental: A poem's meanings and effects are generated through the interplay of form and content. Broadly speaking the form can either work with or against a poem's content. Conventionally a sonnet, for instance, is about love, whereas a limerick is a comic form. A serious love poem in the form of a limerick would be unusual, as would a sonnet about an old man with a beard.

Sometimes poetic form can create an ironic backdrop to highlight an aspect of content. An example would be a formally elegant poem about something monstrous, or a fragile form containing something robust or

vice versa. Wilfred Owen's sonnet, *Anthem for Doomed Youth* might spring to mind as the form of the sonnet sits uneasily with the idea of an anthem and also seems ironic for a poem about war. The artist Grayson Perry uses form in this ironic way. Rather than depicting the sort of picturesque, idealised images we expect of ceramics, Perry's pots and urns depict modern life in bright, garish colours. The urn pictured, for instance, is entitled *Modern Family* and depicts two gay men with a boy who they have presumably adopted. A thrash metal concert inside a church, a philosophical essay via text message, a fine crystal goblet filled with cherryade would be further examples of ironic relationships between message and medium, content and context or form.

Reading form

Put a poem before your eyes. Start off taking a panoramic perspective: Think of the forest, not the trees. Perhaps mist over your eyes a bit.

Don't even read the words, just look at the poem, like at a painting. Is the poem slight, thin, fat, long, short? What is the relation of whiteness to blackness? Why might the poet have chosen this shape? Does it look regular or irregular? A poem about a long winding river will probably look rather different from one about a small pebble, or should do. Unless form is being employed ironically. Now read the poem a couple of times. First time, fast as you can, second time more slowly and carefully. How does the visual layout of the poem relate to what it seems to be about? Does this form support, or create a tension against, the content? Is the form one you recognise, like a sonnet, or is it more open, more irregular like free verse? Usually the latter is obvious from the irregularity of the stanzas, line lengths and lack of metre or rhyme.

As Hurley and O'Neill explain in *Poetic Form: An Introduction*, like genre, form sets expectations: 'In choosing form, poets bring into play associations and expectations which they may then satisfy, modify or subvert'.[1] We've already suggested that if we see a poem is a sonnet or a limerick this recognition will set up expectations about the nature of the poem's content. The same thing works on a smaller level; once we have noticed that a poem's first stanza is a quatrain, we expect it to continue in this neat, orderly fashion. If the quatrain's rhyme scheme is xaxa, xbxb, in which only the second and fourth lines rhyme, we reasonably expect that the next stanza will be xcxc. So, if it isn't we need to consider why.

After taking in the big picture in terms of choice of form in relation to content zoom in: Explore the stanza form, lineation, punctuation, the use of enjambment and caesura. Single line stanzas draw attention to themselves. If they are end-stopped they can suggest isolation, separation. Couplets imply twoness. Stanzas of three lines are called tercets and feature in villanelles and terza rima. On the page, both these forms tend to look rather delicate, especially if separated from each other by the silence of white space. Often balanced through rhyme,

---

[1] Hurley & O'Neill, *Poetic Form, An Introduction*, p.3.

quatrains look a bit more robust and sturdy. Cinquains are swollen quatrains in which the last line often seems to throw the stanza out of balance.

Focus in on specific examples and on points of transition. For instance, if a poem has four regular quatrains followed by a couplet, examine the effect of this change. If we've been ticking along nicely in iambic metre and suddenly trip on a trochee, examine why. Consider regularity. Closed forms of poems, such as sonnets, are highly regular with set rhyme schemes, metre and number of lines. The opposite form is called 'open', the most extreme version of which is free verse. In free verse poems, the poet dispenses with any set metre, rhyme scheme or recognisable traditional form. What stops this sort of poetry from being prose chopped up to look like verse? The care of the design on the page. Hence, we need to focus here on lineation. Enjambment runs over lines and makes connections; caesura pauses a line and separates words. Lots of enjambment generates a sense of the language running away from the speaker. Lots of caesuras generate a halting, hesitant, choppy movement to lines. Opposites, these devices work in tandem and where they fall is always significant in a good poem.

Remember poetic form is never merely decorative. And bear in mind too the fact that the most volatile materials require the strongest containers, or, as Adrienne Rich puts it, 'like asbestos gloves [formalism] allowed me to handle materials I couldn't pick up barehanded'.

Nice to metre...

A brief guide to metre and rhythm in poetry

Why express yourself in poetry? Why read words dressed up and expressed as a poem? What can you get from poetry that you can't from prose? There are many compelling answers to these questions. Here, though, we're going to concentrate on one aspect of the unique appeal of poetry – the structure of sound in poetry. Whatever our stage of education, we are all already sophisticated at detecting and using structured sound. Try reading the following sentences without any variation whatsoever in how each sound is emphasised, and they will quickly lose what essential human characteristics they have. The

 sentences will sound robotic. So, in a sense, we won't be teaching anything

new here. It's just that in poetry the structure of sound is carefully unusually crafted and created. It becomes a key part of what a poem is.

We will introduce a few new key technical terms along the way, but the ideas are straightforward. Individual sounds [syllables] are either stressed [emphasised, sounding louder and longer] or unstressed. As well as clustering into words and sentences for meaning, these sounds [syllables] cluster into rhythmic groups or feet, producing the poem's metre, which is the characteristic way its rhythm works.

In some poems, the rhythm is very regular and may even have a name, such as iambic pentameter. At the other extreme a poem may have no discernible regularity at all. As we have said, this is called free verse. It is vital to remember that the sound in a good poem is structured so that it combines effectively with the meanings.

For example, take a look at these two lines from Marvell's *To his Coy Mistress*:

'But at my back I alwaies hear
Time's winged Chariot hurrying near:'

Forgetting the rhythms for a moment, Marvell is basically saying at this point 'Life is short, Time flies, and it's after us'. Now concentrate on the rhythm of his words.

- In the first line every other syllable is stressed: 'at', 'back', 'al', 'hear'.
- Each syllable before these is unstressed 'But', 'my', 'I', 'aies'.
- This is a regular beat or rhythm which we could write ti TUM / ti TUM / ti TUM / ti TUM , with the / separating the feet. ['Feet' is the technical term for metrical units of sound]
- This type of two beat metrical pattern is called iambic, and because there are four feet in the line, it is tetrameter. So this line is in 'iambic tetrameter'. [Tetra is Greek for four]
- Notice that 'my' and 'I' being unstressed diminishes the speaker, and we are already prepared for what is at his 'back', what he can 'hear' to be bigger than him, since these sounds are stressed.
- On the next line, the iambic rhythm is immediately broken off, since the next line hits us with two consecutive stressed syllables straight off: 'Time's' 'wing'. Because a pattern had been established, when it suddenly changes the reader feels it, the words feel crammed together more urgently, the beats of the rhythm are closer, some little parcels of time have gone missing.

A physical rhythmic sensation is created of time slipping away, running out. This subtle sensation is enhanced by the stress-unstress-unstress pattern of words that follow, 'chariot hurrying'

[TUM-ti-ti, TUM-ti-ti]. So the hurrying sounds underscore the meaning of the words.

14 ways of looking at a poem

 Though conceived as pre-reading exercises, most of these tasks work just as well for revision.

1.   Crunch it [1] – This means re-ordering all of the text in the poem under grammatical headings of nouns, verbs, prepositions and so forth. If this is done before reading the poem for the first time, the students' task is [a] to try to create a poem from this material and [b] to work out what they can about the style and themes of the original poem from these dislocated grammatical aspects. An alternative is to list the words alphabetically and do the same exercise. Re-arranging the poem in grammatical categories after reading can also be a useful analytical task.

2. Crunch it [2] – This is another exercise that can be used as an introductory activity before reading a poem for the first time or as a useful revision task. Rearrange the poem into groupings based on lexico-semantic fields. Show students one group of words at a time, asking them to write down what each group of words might tell us about the poem's themes & style. Alternatively, split the class into small groups and give each one group of words each. Ask them to suggest possible titles for the poem.

3. Crunch it [3] – In this method students have to reduce each line of the poem to one key word. If they do this individually, then in pairs, then as a class, it can facilitate illuminating whole class discussion and bring out different readings. We've applied the cruncher at the end of each of the following essays.

4. Cloze it [aka blankety-blank] – A cloze exercise helps students to focus on specific choices of vocabulary. Blank out a few important words in the first couple of stanzas and as much as you dare of the rest of the poem. Make this task harder as the course goes on. Or use it for revision to see how well the poem's been remembered.

5. Shuffle it – Give students all the lines in the poem but in the wrong order. Their task is to find the right order. Make this a physical exercise; even older pupils like sticking cut up pieces of paper together! Start off with reasonably easy activities. Then make them fiendishly hard.

6. Split it – Before a first reading, post a few key lines from the poem around the classroom, like clues for literary detectives. Arrange the class into small groups. Each group analyses only a few lines. Feedback to the class what they have found out, what they can determine about the poem. Ask them how the information from other groups confirms/ changes their thoughts. Finish by getting them to sequence the lines.

7. Transform it – Turn the poem into something else, a storyboard for a film version, a piece of music or drama, a still image, a collage of images or a piece of performance art. Engage your and their creativity.

8. Switch it – Swap any reference to gender in the poem and the gender of the poet. Change every verb or noun or metaphor or smile in the poem. Compare with the non-doctored version; what's revealed?

9. Pastiche or parody it – Ask students to write a poem in the style of one of the poems from the anthology. Take printed copies in. Add your own and one other poem. See if the students can recognise the published poem from the imitations. A points system can add to the fun.

10. Match it [1] – Ask students to find an analogue for the poem. Encourage them to think metaphorically. If they think Burnside's History is like a thrash metal song by the The Frenzied Parsnips they'll really need to explain how.

11. Match it [2] – Take some critical material on about 5 or 6 poets; there's good stuff on the Poetry by Heart and Poetry Archive websites. Take one poem by each of these poets and a photo. Mix this material up on one page of A3. The students' task is to match the poet to the critical material and to the image. To add to the creative fun you could make up a poem, poet and critical comments.

12. Complete it - Give the students the first few lines of the poem. Their task is to complete it. If they get stuck and plead profusely and if you're feeling especially generous you can give them a few clues, such as the rhyme scheme or the stanza form.

13. Write back - If the poem's a dramatic monologue, change the point of view and write the other character's version of events. What might be the silent thoughts of the woman in *Talking in Bed*? What might the Sexton's lover have to say if he could reply to her poem?

14. Listen to it - Tell the class you're going to read the poem once. Their task is to listen carefully and then write down as much of it as they can remember, working first on their own and then in pairs. Read the poem a second time and repeat the exercise. Discuss what they did and didn't remember.

'Poetry is as much a mode of reading as writing'

DON PATTERSON

Maya Angelou, *Caged Bird*

Bitterness is like a cancer. It eats upon the host.

In her extraordinary autobiographical novel, *I Know Why the Caged Bird Sings,* first published in 1984, the American novelist, singer, actor, political activist and poet, Maya Angelou [1928 – 2014] vividly describes her childhood and teenage years. At the heart of the novel is the warmth of Maya's relationships with close family, especially her brother, Bailey, her sometimes erratic Momma and her formidable grandmother. Around this unit is the society of the black neighbourhood of Stamps, Arkansas, where the bookish Maya was raised. As she grows up, Maya becomes ever more aware of her colour, its social status and of the iniquity of racial segregation: 'A light shade had been pulled down between the Black community and all things white, but one could see through it enough to develop a fear-admiration-contempt'[2]. The novel also reveals that her mother's boyfriend, Mr. Freeman, raped Maya when she was eight years old. After the subsequent trial, having escaped conviction, Mr. Freeman is killed, and, feeling that her words have directly caused his murder, Maya becomes an elective mute for the next five years of her life.

A novel dealing with such a horrific, brutal violation could easily have

---

[2] *I Know Why the Caged Bird Sings,* chapter 8.

become a misery memoir or a novel filled with bitterness, anger and disgust. But Maya Angelou was made of sterner and wiser stuff – somehow she finds a place in her heart to forgive a man who raped her and determines to not let the rape define who she is nor who she will become. Though Angelou experienced first-hand injustice, abuse, cruelty and suffering and understood these things more intimately than anyone would wish, she didn't let that knowledge destroy her. Instead she used it as rocket fuel for her political activism and campaigns for social justice. Remarkably, from her experiences of the harshest, most brutal aspects of human behaviour, she developed an intensely joyous appreciation of the best things in life – love, laughter, friends, nature, beauty, song, art, dancing. As she herself put it in her anthemic poem *Still I Rise*: 'Leaving behind nights of terror and fear / I rise / Into a daybreak that's wondrously clear / I rise'.

Many writers are admirable, even inspiring figures - individuals who go against social norms, sometimes actively fighting against injustices, sometimes just following their own artistic impulses to create, often revealing something new in their writing about the human condition. But few writers would claim to be as inspirational a figure as Maya Angelou. Lifting herself up by the gale-force of her personality and through the tremendous range of her talents, she became a world-renowned writer, a Professor of Literature and the first American poet to read at the inauguration of an American president since Robert Frost in 1963. Moreover, she was also the first female poet to do so and the first black poet do so too.

Look up or google any clip of Maya Angelou talking or being interviewed, such as https://www.youtube.com/watch?v=sr6LMr-rXEc and as well as her sharp critical intelligence, her deep wisdom and understanding of human beings, what comes over is the humour, warmth, kindness and tremendous generosity of her spirit. Maya Angelou was an indefatigable, indomitable, big-hearted human being, a great soul determined to make the world a better, kinder place for everyone, determined to 'just do right'. A truly inspirational writer.

Anger is like fire. It burns all clean.

Obviously, Angelou's poem is constructed on a central contrast between two worlds, those of the free and caged birds. While the free bird treats the world like it's a series of funfair rides and seems to lord it over creation, the caged bird lives trapped within a gothic 'grave of dreams' and can only sing of the sort of freedom the other bird so ostentatiously enjoys. Whereas the free bird is exuberant, in harmony with a natural world that seems designed to serve its purposes, and feels entitled to its privileges, the caged bird is defined by restriction and consequent suffering. For the free bird the natural forces of motion, such as the wind, operate in a comfortably 'soft' manner and the entire world is a gentle floating, sighing, brightly-lit, relaxing, holiday sort of place. The comfortable interaction this bird has with the world around it is conveyed by the fact that even its commerce with the world is easy; the '**trade** winds', are soft. Everything the free bird could wish for seems to be provided; the wind and stream provide transport and food is arranged, nicely plumped - 'fat worms' conveniently are 'waiting' for the bird in an attractive space, a 'dawn-bright lawn', where they can be easily spotted, and devoured. Dawn, of course, symbolically signals hope and new beginnings, associations emphasised by 'bright', and 'lawn' suggests nature domesticated and cultivated for the bird's pleasure and ease. The notion that, presumptuously and perhaps hubristically, the free bird sees the world, and all that's in it, as his own is underlined at the end of each of its stanzas. More precisely, it is the 'sky' the bird names its own – literally above the world and a space associated, of course, with God.

In contrast, the caged bird's world is nightmarishly dark, like a grave,

 and the bird is itself reduced to only to insubstantial darkness, being only a 'shadow'. Angelou employs repetition again at the end of the fifth stanza, this time to underline how the caged bird is further restrained within its prison. Not only is the bird locked within the 'narrow cage' with 'bars', but it is also shackled, 'tied'

and 'clipped', like slaves on slave ships, 'Shadow', of course, implies a dark body and Angelou's use of the emotive word 'scream', rather than a more avian noise such as 'screech', ensures that readers register the human suffering embodied by the bird.

But, as well as such striking differences, these two symbols of the free and caged bird also have things in common, suggesting a deep-rooted and fundamental kinship. Firstly, and most obviously, Angelou uses the same animal as a symbol for both figures. It takes little imagination on the reader's part to substitute white man and black man for the free and caged birds and to think of the two worlds they inhabit as representing the sort of racial segregation Angelou experienced as a child. This raises a couple of interesting questions. What does Angelou gain by using the bird symbol and why does she make her birds male? We'll return to 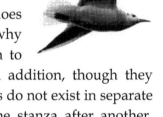 these questions at the end of this essay. In addition, though they contrast so starkly, the worlds of the two birds do not exist in separate universes; rather they are close together, one stanza after another, cheek-by-jowl, separate, but also intermixed.

Another way in which the two worlds are close and alike is how they are arranged in stanzas on the page. Both the first two stanzas have seven lines in total and are comprised of short lines of up to only six words or three beats. On the page they look rather similar. In addition, both the first two stanzas share irregular rhyme patterns and are composed of one sentence that completes itself with a full stop after the last word.

For the first three stanzas *Caged Bird's* sprightly lines are made up of a mixture of dimeters and trimeters. At times the pattern is regular iambic, as in 'and **dips** his **wing**' and 'his **bars** of **rage**' which both have two emphatic stresses. In the last line of each of the first two stanzas the metre lengthens a little into tetrameter:

'and **dares** to **claim** the **sky**'
'So he **o**pens his **throat** to **sing**'

You'll have noticed that there's an extra unstressed syllable at the start of the second example, so that line actually begins with an anapaest. In all the stanzas, Angelou uses this metrical variation from time to time to accelerate the verse a little and generate momentum, most notably in 'on the **back** of the **wind**' and lines such as 'and the **trade** winds **soft**'.

Rhymes and half-rhymes come quickly and often in all the stanzas. Take the first stanza. Here the long open 'ee' of the first line's 'free' runs assonantally through 'leaps' and 'stream' and the short 'i' of 'wind' is carried through 'still', 'dips' and 'wing', while 'rays' assonates with 'claims'. Alliterative patterns further the echoic richness: 'bird' & 'back'; 'free' & 'float'' 'wind' & 'wing', and there's also a run of 'd' sounds linking the whole stanza, from 'bird' via 'wind' and 'ends' to culminate in 'dares'. Coupled with the short lines and swift-running metre, the sound patterning generates in the first stanza a sense of vibrant energy that reflects the bird's freedom, movement and exuberant mood.

Suitably enough, though the lines have the similar lengths and the metre follows a similar pattern, the echoic effects are dampened down in the following two stanzas describing the trapped bird. The difference is also emphasised by the verbs Angelou employs. In the first stanza, for instance, there are four dynamic verbs describing the bird's actions and mood, as it 'leaps', 'floats', 'dips' and 'dares'. Contrastingly, in the second stanza the bird 'stalks', [can seldom] 'see' and 'opens'. Grammatically the caged bird is also a passive subject of another agent – its wings 'are clipped' and its feet 'are tied'.

Same old difference

So, Angelou's poem is characterised by a pattern of both similarity and difference. In both halves of the poem one stanza describing the free bird, for example, is followed by two describing the situation for the caged bird. Each half of the poem also ends with the same stanza repeated. Furthermore, as we have seen, all the stanzas have similar structural arrangements. On the other hand, the third stanza is a line longer than the two preceding it and in the fourth and fifth stanzas the lines are organised differently, stretched out longer to create thicker, shorter stanzas. As the metre's fundamentally the same, the poet could have set the fourth stanza out in the same way as the previous ones:

The free bird thinks
Of another breeze
And the trade winds soft
Through the sighing trees
And the fat worms waiting
On a dawn-light lawn
And he names the sky his own.

What, if anything, does Maya Angelou suggest by changing the way the lines are arranged? Perhaps the fundamental sameness of the structure of the stanzas again implies deeper kinship between things that look superficially very different. Perhaps too she's implying that whatever way anyone might package and try to re-arrange this situation, however much they may try to make it look different on the surface, it's fundamentally the same, constant and unchanging. Another way of saying this is that the same injustice and oppression can be found in different looking stanzas, i.e. in different contexts, such as different times and places. The outside might look different, but inside things are just the same.

His tune is heard

Angelou's poem could be in danger of presenting a seemingly hopeless situation: The free and caged birds live entirely different lives, one enjoying a world of pleasure, ease and freedom, the other caged, restrained and screaming. Counterbalancing this bleakness is the fact that the caged bird 'sings'. We might think of slave songs, Gospel, Blues, Jazz and many other musical forms that have been born out of the historical suffering of black people. Such music has palpable power, authenticity, what the Spanish call duende, because it comes from such extremes of human experience. In darkness the brighter a light seems; to those oppressed the more powerful are dreams of freedom. Not only that, but Angelou makes it clear that the music will escape the cage, that it will carry, and carry far. This music will communicate and find an audience – it 'is heard', even on the 'distant hill' – holding out the possibility of future liberation. Note too the use of the present tense, 'is heard'. Perhaps there won't be too long a wait for freedom.

For me, like most of Maya Angelou's writing, *Caged Bird* has duende – a deep authenticity and soulfulness informed by sadness and animated by passionate intensity. Why does Angelou use the bird symbol? And why does a feminist writer use a male bird? Well, birds are universally associated with freedom and, of course, with singing. Hence they are also a traditional symbol for poets/ artists. The bird symbol also universalises the situation, allowing people in different contexts of  oppression and injustice to identify with it. In this way, *Caged Bird* does not only apply to solely black experience, but to anyone anywhere who feels oppressed and any context where there is a huge divide between people in power and people without power. Perhaps, that is also the reason behind Angelou's surprising choice of male birds. Would it be problematic for a feminist writer to imply that white women were free as birds and arrogantly thought of the entire natural world as their own dominion? Yes, probably. And it wouldn't have rung true.

Historically at least, it is white men who have occupied this heightened and privileged position. So, the bird has to be male. As Rudyard Kipling once wrote, 'if you can fill the unforgiving minute / with sixty seconds' worth of distance run / yours is the earth and everything that's in it / and what is more, you'll be a man, my son'. What was left for his daughters and for people from different cultures, the poet didn't say.

Caged Bird crushed:

FREE – WIND – FLOATS – CURRENT – DIPS – SUN'S – DARES – BUT – CAGE – THROUGH – RAGE – CLIPPED – TIED – SING – CAGED – FEARFUL – UNKNOWN – LONGED – HEARD – HILL – CAGED – FREEDOM – BREEZE – TRADE – FAT – OWN – GRAVE – SCREAM – CLIPPED – OPENS – SINGS – FEARFUL – THINGS – STILL – TUNE – DISTANT – CAGED – FREEDOM.

If you enjoyed *Caged Bird*, try *Still I Rise*, which you can find easily in print form on the internet, or you can watch Maya Angelou reading it herself. And Angelou's autobiographical novel *I Know Why the Caged Bird Sings* is powerful, profound and inspiring.

Norman Nicholson, *Rising Five*

Had we but space and time [and an infinitely patient reader], there'd be so much to say and do with Nicholson's virtuoso poem. Presenting  it the first time to a class I'd want to bring out a couple of its most distinctive features and help students to appreciate them. Firstly, arrange it on the page without the curious lineation, such as the great blank spaces of time after 'more', 'fruit', 'light', and the smaller spaces before 'And' and after 'night'. Secondly, cut the last stanza of the poem and ask students to predict its contents. A really ambitious task would be to ask them to have a go at writing the last stanza themselves. Once they've tried to complete the poem in either prose or verse, show them all but the last two lines and again ask the students to try to predict these. If the students write their closing lines on pieces of paper and pass them to you and you write down Nicholson's, you can make a game of this by reading out each possible ending and then voting for the one they think is the best and/or the poet's.

What's most striking about this poem? Three aspects, in particular, immediately stand out:

1.   Its Keatsian lyrical richness and lush tones

2. The unusual way it's set out on the page typographically
3. The brilliant way Nicholson riffs on a local dialect phrase, 'rising five', extending and developing this in surprising ways, broadening it into a philosophical reflection on human nature.

Mellow fruitfulness

Inevitably as a Cumbrian poet who characteristically used an earthy, man-speaking-to-men idiom, Nicholson has often been compared to his great predecessor, William Wordsworth. And *Rising Five* is distinctly Romantic. It features a conversation with a young child, it's set in the countryside and it focuses our attention on the natural world – the scenery, the sky, the light. However, though thematically this poem may echo Wordsworth, in terms of style it seems to me to be more Keatsian. This is particularly the case in the poem's most sumptuously lyrical section, which comes in the second stanza where Nicholson describes the fecund processes of nature. Here the poet orchestrates a multitude of sonic and semantic devices to generate richly textured, richly musical verse.

In its second line, for instance, Nicholson intensifies the poem's rhyming with the internal rhyme of 'bubbled and doubled' and enriches it further by combining plosive alliteration of 'b' sounds with a run of 'd' sounds and assonantal 'u's:

'**B**u**bb**led and **d**oubled; **b**uds unbuttoned; shoot'

Read it aloud and the line has a tangible physical bubbliness. Note too how the caesura creates a pause before the verb, or potentially noun, 'shoot'. With very different sonic qualities to the rest of the line and a long 'o' vowel, the sound of the word 'shoot' is made especially onomatopoeic here. In addition, liquidly 'l' sounds flow through the stanza, from 'cells' to 'bubbled' and 'doubled' to 'frills' and 'swilled' [a word, as we shall discuss in a moment, that itself suggests water].

Swishing sibilance - 'cells', 'spring', buds', 'shoot', 'stem', 'shook', 'creases' and so forth - flows through the lines. In fact, almost all the words in this stanza are woven into its dense sonic wash. Take the ordinary, innocuous and colourless adjective 'every'. 'Every' is not a word that would normally draw much attention or interest in a poem. However, here its first syllable echoes 'stem' in the previous line and its second chimes with '<u>creases</u>', 'tree', 'green' and '<u>season</u>'. Check the stanza and you'll find an abundance of other varieties of alliteration and assonance.

Working alongside the multiple echoic effects, imagery, of both the sensory and figurative varieties, adds semantic richness: The 'cells of spring' recall Keats' 'clammy cells' in *To Autumn* and conveys the idea of confinement preceding exuberant release and growth. The Keatsian echo is amplified by the sensory imagery, specifically tactile and aural, as Nicholson describes cells which 'bubbled', as if nature is boiling with

energy. In the same stanza the poet compares plants to clothing, with 'buds' becoming 'unbuttoned' and stems having their 'creases' 'shook out' from their 'frills' – everything is moving, opening up and stretching outwards. A sense of dynamism and liberated energy animates the lines. The use of the verb 'swilled' is interesting, for example. Normally the word is a synonym for wash or rinse. Here it picks up the earlier 'l' sounds, gives the trees' greenness a synesthetic liquidyness and adds to the sense of fecundity [we tend to use lots of water when we 'swill' something and swilling implies vigour].

Space and time

What is the effect, or the point, if any, of the poem's gaps and its very distinctive shape on the page? For example, there's a great, long, silent space after 'more' and the colon that tells us the following words will exemplify a point, before, finally, we reach 'not four', stuck out on the end of the line. The gap creates a dramatic pause, isolates those two short emphatic words and gives them greater force. The same effect is created at the end of the second stanza. Once we get to 'Not May' we anticipate the completing half of the line, especially as we have already seen this pattern in the first stanza. Comedians often talk about the timing of a joke and Nicholson controls the timing of our reading so that we have a little moment of anticipation before the equivalent of the punchline arrives. The poem then speeds up with two further riffs on the 'not x, but rising y' refrain. Whereas the first two stanzas work their way to this refrain, in its middle section the poem dispenses with any introductory matter and cuts to the chase of its key idea. There's an intensification, a sense that we're building to some sort of climax, not least because the lines shorten and full rhymes come more swiftly one after another. The loosening and opening up of the form also exposes the words to more white space, so that they almost seem to be floating in air. This typography also aligns with the shift from the materiality of the opening two stanzas to the abstract ideas of light and time. In addition, the lay-out exaggerates the eye's movements from left to right, a visual equivalent of the binary 'not x, but y' notion.

There's a return to solidity in the final stanza and a return too in the subject matter. Again there is nature and the boy and the solid, material world. Hence this stanza feels summative, the poet building to a conclusion drawn from his earlier observations. Again, Nicholson invites us to anticipate the ending, particularly with the introduction of the word 'rot' suddenly darkening the mood. Isolation of the phrase 'but **ris**ing **dead**' makes it suitably stark, and the heavy, strikingly sombre effect is lent greater weight through both the stress pattern and the fact that this is the only fully rhyming end word in the stanza.

Rising Five

The poet takes the boy's casual insistence that he's not four, but 'rising five' and applies the idea in several other contexts, extending and deepening its meaning, eventually taking it a long way from its original context. Nicholson finds the same pattern of perception when considering the months, day and night and time itself, suggesting it might be a universal way of seeing things or stitched into the fabric of our perceptions. To appreciate the linguistic brilliance, try coming up with your own 'not x, but rising y' formulations. 'Not black, but rising white'? No, doesn't work. 'Not good, but rising bad'. Nope. Certainly, it's trickier than it first appears. In the final stanza Nicholson follows his perception to its ultimate conclusion, taking the poem into more profound territory. The description of 'new buds' pushing 'old leaves from the bough' implies harsh, Darwinian competition and the following brilliant simile of the boy casually discarding his sweet wrappers suggests our thoughtless carelessness, the way we are inclined to waste our lives and/or forget our past. The urgently pressing sense of the future, it seems, can prevent us from appreciating the present, and the worst consequences of this can be that our fear of death, 'the grave in the bed', stops us from appreciating life, and we become numbed to the beauty of the world, not much more than living dead.

Rising Five crunched:

RISING – COILS – HEAD – BRIMFUL – MEADOW – ALIVE – MORE – NOT – FIVE – CELLS – UNBUTTONED – OUT – SWILLED – BLOSSOMING – FRUIT – MAY – JUNE – SKY – LIGHT – DAY – NIGHT – NOW – SOON – NEW – YOUTH – FLOWER – FRUIT – ROT – GRAVE – LIVING – DEAD.

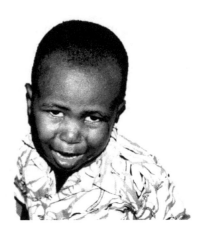

Mervyn Morris, *Little Boy Crying*

The quick slap struck

Jamaican poet and literary professor Mervyn Morris' poem raises difficult questions about a parent's right to discipline their child and, in particular, whether the use of such violence can ever be justified. While we should be careful about being too judgemental about people from other nationalities, cultures and times, and remain aware that readers from different backgrounds will feel differently about this issue, to many modern readers, I expect, Morris' poem fails as a piece of self-justification. Though the poet shows empathy for his son's feelings and claims his actions were, in fact, necessary via a rather cryptic aphorism at the end of the poem, arguably this is not enough to justify or excuse his use of violence on a small child.

The first stanza is a vivid portrait of the physical impact of the slap on the child. In particular, Morris focuses on visual and aural transformations: 'Laughter' becomes animalistic 'howls'; the boy's 'relaxed' body becomes 'tight'; 'bright eyes' turn to 'tears'. There's an implication that to some extent the boy's reaction might be calculated to arouse pity in his father: 'you stand *angling*...'. This impression is strengthened in the last stanza when the boy's tears as described as 'easy'. The reference to the boy feeling 'spite' also seeks to tip the balance of the reader's sympathies a little away from him. Depending on the readers' point of view, these details can be read either as cynical pieces of self-justification or examples of astute psychological realism.

More empathetically, Morris switches perspectives in the second stanza, seeing the scene from a perspective that doesn't quite fully commit to the child's point of view. This seems a protective strategy as much as a stylistic one. Probably it would have been much harder emotionally for the poet to refer to himself as 'me' rather than the distancing and more comforting pronoun 'him'. Nevertheless, the poet is able to see the situation through his son's eyes. These child's eyes turn the admonishing father into a monster from a fairy tale, an 'ogre' and 'grim giant', one who will face the sort of revenge cruel giants in fairy tales deserve and invariably receive. Whereas the poet imagines his son's revenge fantasy springing from intense, undiluted emotion ['you hate him'] he assumes that his son would see him as emotionless. 'Empty of feeling', rather than angry, suggests that the 'slap' may

have been delivered in a calm and deliberate manner. A contrast is being developed here between the father and the son's use, or potential use, of violence.

Spare the rod and spoil the child

There's an inconsistency in the way the poet imagines how his son interprets his behaviour. On the one hand, Morris describes himself through his son's eyes as being without feeling, but, at other times he describes himself as 'cruel' and as 'this *fierce* man'. Perhaps this inconsistency conveys the idea that the small child doesn't really know how to read his father's behaviour or how to understand his motivation, or it may be that by 'feeling' Morris means feelings of sympathy. Certainly, the poet believes that, in time, the child will come to 'understand' the ambivalence and doubts, the 'wavering' the father felt and by extension come to appreciate why he did what he did. Though he might have appeared to be an emotionless 'ogre', in fact, beneath this 'mask' the father was 'hurt' - the boy's tears are very painful, they 'scald' him, and he 'longs' to make his son happy again. But he cannot, he believes, because to do so would be to 'ruin the lessons' the boy 'should learn'.

Interestingly, Morris doesn't include the behaviour that earnt this piece of physical punishment. For many readers, no doubt, no poor behaviour justifies hitting a child, but we may have understood more, if not excused, the punishment if we knew how severe the misdemeanour had been. The fact that the poet doesn't include this information suggests that it wasn't a significant detail to him.

Poets often insist that poems resist reductive paraphrasing. Nevertheless, Morris' poem exemplifies and really boils down to the well-known aphorism from *Proverbs* quoted on the previous page. Rather than recycling this biblical phrase, the poet re-formulates and sets it out on its own line as a sort of moral to be drawn from the poem's didactic narrative. The phrasing makes the line a little lyrical and Zen-sounding, lending the conventional sentiment the feeling of deep, resonant wisdom. Generally, in this poem, Morris makes his verse sound like slightly intensified speech. For instance, though most of the lines are pentameters, there's no regular pattern of iambs or trochees. Occasionally lines do fall into regular metrical patterns, such as the iambic tetrameter of 'you **can**not **under**stand, not **yet**' which lends the sentiment a kind of rhythmic authority. But at other times the metre is scrambled. Similarly, though there are a few rhymes, they crop up in odd places. For example, 'spite', 'tight' and 'bright' from the opening stanza. Here and there we can also spot patches of alliteration.

The final line, however, is probably the most tangibly crafted in the whole poem, with several poetic techniques applied to make it resonate in the reader's mind when they turn their attention elsewhere. The metre, for example, is a regular pentameter whose stresses fall with suitably emphatic weight:

'You *must* not *ma*ke a pl**a**ything **of** the r**ain**'[3]

In addition, alliteration adds further stress to the first two monosyllables, and assonance takes over and has the same impact as the line develops. The central verb 'make' links the line together by echoing the 'm' of 'must' and the 'a' sound of 'play' and 'rain'. The overall effect is that the sounds amplify the sense, giving the line a unified quality and lyrical resonance.

Ambiguous use of the second-person pronoun, 'you' makes it unclear, however, whether this a general principle to be drawn by the reader – you must not toy with and trivialise something natural/ you must not interfere with a natural process etc., or whether this is the specific lesson the boy was meant to learn. If the latter, it seems a rather hard-to-grasp and elliptical thing for a three-year-old child to learn. Perhaps the absence of a colon at the end of the penultimate line tips the balance of interpretation towards the former, universal lesson about the apparent necessity of physical punishment. As with the avoidance of the first person 'me', there's something of an evasion here, using a poetic-sounding, difficult to pin-down phrase to try to justify or excuse the 'educative' use of violence.

Overall it seems the poem is pulling rather in two directions. In part it wants to be a clear didactic parable, building its narrative in order to deliver a moral message or truth. But, another part of the poem seems uneasy with this and expresses more ambivalence about the use of violence. Hence, for example, the shift into the child's perspective. However, if the poet had been entirely four-square behind the poem's message, he could easily have shown this by writing more directly and unashamedly in the first person.

---

[3] For readers especially interested in prosody [and who isn't?] we should add that, arguably, 'of' is not, in fact, stressed. If this is the case, then the poet is employing a technique called pyrrhic substitution, whereby, by diminishing the stress on 'of', the stress on 'rain' is increased, or so the argument would go.

Little Boy Crying crushed:

SPITE – HOWLS – TIGHT – THREE-YEAR-OLD – TEARS – ANGLING – SLAP – OGRE – CRUEL – VICTIM – HATE – CHOPPING – TRAP – UNDERSTAND – HURT – MASK – FIERCE – ANYTHING – LESSONS – MUST.

Sujata Bhatt, *Muliebrity*

Devoid of stanzas, with irregular length lines, lacking regular metrical or rhyme structures, Bhatt's poem can be classed as free verse. What distinguishes a free verse poem from prose chopped up and arranged to look like poetry? Not much, in not very good free verse poems, in my opinion. Clearly a key difference between verse and prose is the former's use of lineation. In prose, like this you're reading now, sentences stretch to the borders of the page, whereas in poems they terminate rarely more than half way across. Hence the choice of when to cut a sentence into two lines is crucial in free verse poems, and it is one productive way of evaluating how successful these poems are. If the lines are not cut at the most effective points, or the lineation makes no difference to how the words are read [especially the pacing and rhythm of reading], what has been the point of arranging them on the page to look, only superficially, like a poem?

 So, this time your task, or that of your class, is to try to work out the lineation of Bhatt's poem. I would also withhold, for now, the title of the poem so that once they've completed this lineation task, students can try to come up with their own appropriate title.

I have thought so much about the girl who gathered cow-dung in a wide, round basket along the main road passing by our house and the Radhavallabh temple in Maninagar. I have thought so much about the way she moved her hands and her waist and the smell of cow-dung and road-dust and wet canna lilies, the smell of monkey breath and freshly washed clothes and the dust from crows' wings which smells different – and again the smell of cow-dung as the girl scoops it up, all these smells surrounding me separately and simultaneously – I have thought so much but have been unwilling to use her for a metaphor, for a nice image – but most of all unwilling to forget her or to explain to anyone the greatness and the power glistening through her cheekbones each time she found a particularly promising mound of dung –

How did you or your class do? My guess is that you'll find it pretty difficult to anticipate where some of the lines are cut, not least because they vary so much in length in Bhatt's poem, from eleven words to just three, albeit the last line seems deliberately incomplete. Pay closer attention to the poem's lineation and we can better appreciate some of the poet's choices. The pause after the first line, for instance, creates a tiny contemplative moment for the reader akin to the poet's reflective mood. Having 'girl' at the end of the line makes the word stand out and isolates it, just as, for the poet, this girl has stood out. The lineation of the following three lines break the depiction into separate sections – the girl with the basket; the main road; the temple - and come to an end with a full-stop, a natural division. This arrangement helps too to lend greater emphasis to the repetition of 'I have thought', a repetition that conveys how this girl has continued to preoccupy the poet. The rest of the line could easily have ended on 'way', but again, Bhatt leaves reference to the girl, this time just 'she', dangling, waiting for the enjambment to carry the sentence into the next line. In the following lines the poet lists the various smells – with the word 'smell' appearing in each line. The phrase 'I have thought so much' appears for the third time, but this time Bhatt's arrangement moves it to the second half of its line. This is significant, because again there's a pause as if for thought at the end of the line, and the change of direction in Bhatt's thinking, signalled by the conjunction 'but', is given stronger emphasis. By placing 'metaphor' at the end of the line the crucial idea that the poet wishes to be faithful to this girl and not 'use her' for some fancy poetic technique or convert her into something she isn't is underscored. Similarly, the reader is given a little nudge to notice the contextually surprising adjective 'greatness' and, in a final use of a significant pause, Bhatt creates an intentionally bathetic effect by leaving 'promising' dangling in the air before bringing it bumping down to earth with 'mound of dung'.

Unwilling to use metaphor

True to her word, Bhatt has composed a poem about this cow-dung gathering girl using only simple, literal, non-metaphorical language.

Muliebrity features no figurative language and, though there is reference to exotic smells, this is not really sensory imagery, as these smells are not evoked or described. The main characteristic of the language is its repetitiveness. As we've seen, the word 'smell' is used five times in close proximity, with the phrase 'the smell of cow-dung' used twice. 'I have thought so much' is repeated three times and the adjective 'unwilling' is used twice in consecutive lines. In addition, each of the poem's two sentences begin with the same phrase and a third of the poem's lines begin with the co-ordinating conjunction, 'and'. Clearly, the poet wished the poem to sound ordinary and prosaic, like natural, everyday speech and not heightened or refined or musical. In this way the down-to-earth style of the poem matches its lowly subject.

The second sentence is extraordinarily long and very loosely knit together. Grammatically it's a simple sentence, comprising a chain of co-ordinated clauses linked by the multiple uses of the simplest conjunctions, 'and' and 'but'. In the latter half of the sentence connecting dashes take over are used rather than more solid and separating full stops, a feature that underlines the way all these different things are connected and of equal importance in the poet's mind. The looseness of the structure creates the impression of spontaneous thought and conveys the excitement of the poet as she remembers another thing and another thing and another thing. It is as if her mind is carried away by a flood of vivid memories.

Glistening in the mind's eye

What was it, exactly, about this specific girl that so entranced the poet's imagination? It's difficult to say, exactly, because Bhatt tells us quite explicitly that she is 'unwilling' to explain to 'anyone' why she sees 'greatness' in this humble girl. Around two hundred years earlier the Romantic poet, William Wordsworth, provided his readers with a little more assistance in his series of poems about lonely, ordinary men and women engaged in hard agricultural work. Characteristically Wordsworth emerges from his interactions with humble rural folk, such as a solitary female reaper working in a Highland vale or an old man gathering leeches by the edge of an isolated pool, with a greater admiration for the stoical qualities they exhibit, their industry, fortitude, perseverance, their ability to cope with their isolation and so forth. Indeed, Wordsworth called his poem about an ancient leech-gatherer *Resolution and Independence*, which gives even the sleepiest of readers an interpretive nudge.

Bhatt's poem, it seems to me, is written in this Romantic vein. Wordsworth also famously aimed to write in a plain, unadorned, unfancy style, like a man speaking to men as he put it, and a key point in his poems is how his memories of these emblematic figures linger in his imagination. Bhatt admires the humbleness of the girl and the intense way she carries out her repetitive and mundane task. The poet admires the fact that the girl seems totally concentrated on what she is doing, even though the work is so monotonous and distinctly physically unappealing. The girl also works independently, it seems. Bhatt appreciates too the fact that the girl can still feel a thrill 'each time' she discovers something 'particularly promising', even in a pile of cow-shit! For Wordsworth, the solitary reaper and the leech-gatherer provided analogues for the work of the sort of rooted-in-the-soil poet he said he wished to be. Perhaps, modestly, Bhatt also sees an image of herself as a writer at work reflected in this girl. Doesn't a writer shift through the dung of everyday experience to try to extract the most promising bits and get excited when they chance upon linguistic nuggets? Don't writers have to work through the dung of their own drafts to find the golden bits they can polish and publish? Bhatt's description of the girl perhaps also expresses some wish-fulfilment – the girl is transformed by her discovery, made radiant and great and has 'power' – all things writer's may feel they have whilst in the throes of composition. But rewards they only rarely recieve in the real world.

Perhaps there's another dimension too to the poet's preoccupation and identification with this girl. Sujata Bhatt is an Indian poet who studied in both England and the USA and who now lives in Germany and is married to a German. She is also a poet who writes in English and Gujarati, often combining the two languages within a single poem. *Muliebrity* was published in her first collection of poems, *Brunziem* in 1988 a collection which centres on a return to her home in India after ten years abroad. In this sense, the Indian identity of the girl, her work and the scene of which she is part is significant to the poet's identification with her. As Bhatt has  herself written 'I never left home / I carried it away with me' just as, in her mind, she carried the image of this girl. This identification and empathy might also appear more radical when considered in the light of the Indian caste system.

The solitary cow-dung gatherer

Such might have been the title perhaps, if Wordsworth had lived in India, in recent times, and written this poem. Surprisingly, and at odds with the style of the poem itself, Bhatt avoids a merely informative, descriptive, down-to-earth title. Instead she opts for something more refined and elevated; a rather highfalutin sounding, Latinate abstract noun. That the word is uncommon and probably unfamiliar to many readers is signalled by the fact that CIE thinks it needs glossing. If readers are feeling uncharitable, they may conclude that the poet is trying to dress up her somewhat plain, unassuming poem just a little in order to lend it in a sense of profundity and universality. Certainly, the title suggests that the poet feels this particular woman is an emblem of womanhood in general. Or does the muliebrity refer instead or, perhaps as well, to the observing writer, who expresses admiration and empathy for even the very lowliest of girls doing the very lowliest of work? Is the poet suggesting, perhaps, that such deep empathy is fundamentally a female quality?

Muliebrity squeezed:

THOUGHT – COW-DUNG – OUR – MANINAGAR – MUCH – MOVED – SMELL – MONKEY – DUST – AGAIN – SURROUNDING – THOUGHT – METAPHOR – UNWILLING – GREATNESS – POWER – PROMISING – DUNG.

William Wordsworth, *She Dwelt Among the Untrodden Ways*

This short poem, Romantic in both senses of that word, lends itself well

to an unscrambling exercise. It has a bouncy, ballad metre, alternating lines of tetrameter and trimeter, three regular quatrains, as well as a cross rhyme scheme. The phrasing of the poem also works in neatly patterned pairs. Such regularity should be a big help to the unscramblers. Perhaps let your class have a go at sorting out the correct order before informing them of any or all of these formal features... [A helpful tactic is for them to try to ascertain the poem's final line.] If, after a while, the class are struggling, then give them clues, such as the information above, or even the first line.

Is shining in the sky.
And very few to love:
The difference to me!
A violet by a mossy stone
A Maid whom there were none to praise
She dwelt among the untrodden ways
- Fair as a star, when only one

She lived unknown, and few could know
When Lucy ceased to be;
Beside the springs of Dove,
But she is in her grave, and, oh,
Half hidden from the eye!

Well-trodden ways

If you're reading this book from start to finish, you'll know that we've just been citing Wordsworth's work in relation to Sujata Bhatt's poem *Muliebrity*. In particular we discussed Wordsworth's valorisation of ordinary, solitary workers doggedly going about their business, and the lasting impression they made on the poet's thinking. As with Bhatt's poem, *She Dwelt Among the Untrodden Ways* focuses on a solitary female character from an obscure and humble background, and also like Bhatt's poem, conveys the poet's intense feeling for this woman. In contrast to *Muliebrity*, Wordsworth's poem is, of course, a love poem from a man to, or about, a woman and it is set in England, probably, as the reference to 'Dove' [presumably Wordsworth's home Dove Cottage] indicates, in the Lake District where the poet was born.

Two hundred or so years after Wordsworth it probably doesn't seem a very edgy move to celebrate a lowly, impoverished character and to make them the subject of a high art form, a poem. But in the late eighteenth century this was an extremely radical thing to do. As a young man Wordsworth, along with fellow political radicals, had been inspired by the politics of the French Revolution [1789-1799] and, in particular, the promise it seemed to hold of sweeping away old, corrupt regimes and ushering in a fairer, more just, more democratic society. Wordsworth travelled to France, had a relationship with a French woman [who bore him a child] and returned to England. However, it soon transpired that the revolution was a horribly false dawn and the dictatorship of a corrupt monarchy was being replaced by another form of dictatorship. As news filtered through to England of the bloody massacres carried out in the name of justice and of murderous infighting among the revolutionary leaders that left nobody safe from the guillotine, fervour for the revolution even among English radicals cooled.

Though repulsed by the savage violence and disorder of the French Revolution and chastened by his experiences, Wordsworth did not give up the hope of helping to form a better world. But he concluded that the methods for reaching the brighter future must be more gradual and less violent. What was needed, he believed, was a radical transformation of the English political psyche, and art would be the vehicle delivering this transformation. And more specifically the art of

poetry. But not the poetry of the previous generation of poets, the Augustans, which Wordsworth thought had grown stale, complacent and overly stylised. To move hearts and minds what was needed was a new radical kind of poetry, a poetry more earthy, rooted in the way people actually speak, plainer and more immediately striking. This poetry would also be emotive, dealing with topics ordinary people could relate to and feel strongly about, in forms drawn from songs. Outlined in the introduction to the book he co-wrote with his fellow radical and friend, Samuel Taylor Coleridge, *The Lyrical Ballads* [1798], Wordsworth delivered this new poetry in works such as his short hybrid lyric poem *She Dwelt Among the Untrodden Ways*. Whether or not his artistic enterprise achieved its political objectives we'll leave for political historians to decide.

Untrodden ways

Wordsworth is keen to emphasise that the beauty he has discovered and been enraptured by was located in an obscure setting. For example, the poem's title is repeated in its first line and there is also a little metrical stumble on the adjective 'untrodden' that draws our attention to it sonically. The first two feet of the first line are regular iambs: 'She **dwelt among**' and the next syllable 'the' is unstressed, implying that the iambic pattern is going to continue smoothly. However, to fit the line into completely regular iambic tetrameter we'd have to stress untrodden as '**un**trodden' and also not stress 'ways'. Doesn't this feel like we're forcing the words, contorting them, into the metre? The more natural stress must be 'untro**dd**en **ways**'. The effect of the metrical irregularity is that the 'un' part of the adjective carries a little more emphasis than it normally would, and Wordsworth gives it a further little sonic push through preceding it with half-rhyming 'am**ong**'. [If you doubt whether this stumbling effect was deliberate, consider how easily Wordsworth could have avoided it, regularising and smoothing the line's metre by simply cutting the otherwise unnecessary definite article 'the'.]

In the next lines, in straightforward terms, he informs us that hardly anyone knew this woman: 'there were none to praise' and 'very few to love' her. These tender thoughts are emphasised in similarly unadorned style and phrasing in the third stanza: 'She lived unknown, and few could know'. In the middle stanza Wordsworth uses a metaphor, comparing the peasant woman to a flower 'half **hidden** from

the eye'. Of course, the poet could have picked any woodland flower to convey the idea that something beautiful might grow hidden away somewhere obscure and remain unappreciated. But it is, of course, significant that Wordsworth uses a violet. In Classical Literature the violet is associated with the goddesses Aphrodite and Persephone. Hence it has come to be associated with both love and death. Partly this must be to with the violet's short life, its brief flowering in spring and its purple, blood-like colour. It is also a precise symbol for Lucy because it tends to grow in shady, out-of-the-way places. In addition, the phrase 'shrinking violet' is still in use today and suggests someone who is rather withdrawn, shy, modest; qualities we might guess Lucy possessed.

In literature, violets also commonly connote faithfulness in love.[4]

Quietly, this violet grows by an unfeeling, inanimate 'stone', not something liable to appreciate the flower's delicate and fragile beauty. And the fact that the stone it/she grows by is 'mossy' further underlines its/Lucy's underappreciated, uncared for, out-of-the-wayness. It is also entirely appropriate that Wordsworth employs natural imagery to describe his beloved who is a country girl. As well as being like a violet, he says she is as 'fair as a star' 'shining in the sky' [a simile echoing the name 'Lucy' which is associated with starlight]. Suggesting beauty and fate, the star simile also adds to the sense of her isolation and remoteness.

Perhaps there is something rather idealised, reductive and even stereotypical about Wordsworth's depiction of this woman. However apposite it may be in this particular instance, comparing a woman to a flower is hardly an original metaphor and, arguably, diminishes and dehumanises her. Ditto the star image. Moreover, Wordsworth concentrates on the woman's external beauty, with little apparent interest in or knowledge of her character. We do learn that she is a 'Maid' and clearly the capitalisation of this word signals that it carries more significance than otherwise might be expected. For contemporary readers the label 'maid' would have indicated virginity and hence suggests purity and chaste virtue. As we've already noted, the violet image also contains within it ideas of modesty and shyness. Furthermore, she is described as 'fair', an adjective that suggests beauty but also virtue. As he did through the capitalisation of 'Maid', the poet draws our attention to the word 'fair', this time through metrical patterning. Scan the poem's lines and you'll spot their almost uniform regularity. Such regularity makes deviation more noticeable and significant. We've already discussed the other instance of irregularity, the adjective 'untrodden' [at great length you might think] and in the

---

[4] For more detail on the symbolism of violets see Michael Ferber's *A Dictionary of Literary Symbols*, pp. 224-6.

second instance Wordsworth simply reverses the first metrical foot, turning it into a trochee and then resuming in iambic pattern, '**fair** as a **star**, when **only one**'. In these ways, it could be argued, Lucy is presented as an unthreatening male fantasy - a fair, chaste, passive maiden, all the more appealing for being undiscovered by other men.

Perhaps too, we might tentatively suggest that the male poet rather appropriates Lucy's quiet tragedy for his own purposes. Sure, he may want the reader to empathise with Lucy, to some extent, but he also wants to take the credit for discovering her beauty. Doesn't spotting her indicate his acute poetic sensibility and sharp aesthetic eye? Moreover, somewhat egotistically, the poem ends with a pretty unsubtle invitation for us to feel most pity for the poet's loss: 'and, oh, the difference to **me!**'. Note too that rather melodramatic exclamation mark - a full-stop might have been more appropriately sombre. A more sympathetic reading might counter that the poet is merely indicating his devastation at the death of someone he loved so much [though, in fact, literary scholars remain unsure about whether Lucy was a real person or just a literary device].

Lyrical ballad

The form of Wordsworth's poem is interesting. Metrically the poem is written as a ballad, a form derived from folk traditions rather than from high art. Arranged in quatrains, the lines alternate between tetrameter and trimeter, i.e. four and three beat lines, with a cross-rhyme scheme of mostly full rhymes. Predominantly the lines run along iambic lines, with one significant deviation, as we've noted. The switch from four beats to three beats, with shorter second lines, creates a subtle falling away quality, a dying cadence, well-matched to the gently melancholic, elegiac tone. There is also a notable pattern of the lines falling into twos, most obviously in the middle stanza. This adds to this trailing off effect and also reflects the two people in the relationship. However, the poem can also be classified as a lyric, as it expresses strong emotions in the first-person voice. Bringing this to mind, we should notice that Wordsworth withholds reference to himself until the last word of the last line, an unusual strategy in a lyric poem. Only at the very end does the poet employ the first first-person pronoun 'me'. Whether this expresses a delicate deference to Lucy's suffering or claims the empathy in the end for the poet himself we'll leave you to decide. Certainly, we should be able to concur that withholding the lyrical 'I' increases its emotional impact.

Whatever we think of Wordsworth's depiction of Lucy - whether the poet innovated stylistically within an aesthetic tradition of appreciation of female beauty by celebrating such a lowly figure, or whether he stands guilty of repeating reductive and clichéd images of docile, passive and chaste femininity, we might agree that he wrote a gently tender poem using ordinary, down-to-earth language. A poem intelligible to most readers and one that expresses melancholic emotions with lyrical poignancy. It's a slight, fragile poem on the page, only twelve lines long, surrounded by a lot of white. A very suitable form for its subject.

She Dwelt Among the Untrodden Ways crunched:

UNTRODDEN – DOVE – MAID – LOVE – VIOLET – HIDDEN – FAIR – SHINING – UNKNOWN – LUCY – GRAVE – ME.

James K. Baxter, *Farmhand*

The wanderer

It seems that New Zealand poet and playwright, James K. Baxter [1926-1972] lived a short, restless, searching sort of life. Something of an artistic child prodigy with a keen interest in mysticism, Baxter had his first collection of poetry published at just eighteen years old. A little later the poet started, but failed to finish a degree course, fell into alcoholism in his twenties and by his thirties had become an ardent Christian. When he converted from Anglicanism to Catholicism it seems to have put a severe strain on his marriage. Having worked in various jobs scratching a meagre living he won an award to visit India in 1958 and returned with a sharper sense of the social injustices of his homeland and a determination to address them in his writing. Inspired by a dream in his forties, Baxter gave up a university academic career to join a Maori settlement, taking on a tribal name and identity. The only possession the poet took with him, apparently, was his Bible. In his later years, he lived an austere existence, helping the poor and people addicted to drugs and speaking and writing about the social injustices he witnessed first-hand around him. Years of harsh, hard living and hard living conditions, caught up with Baxter who died from illness aged just 46.

According to the *Oxford Companion to Modern Poetry*, Baxter was a 'self-styled figure of the 'wilderness' who always saw the artist as a tribesman cut off from his tribe'.[5] Clearly this fits with the poet's depiction of, and empathy for, the lonely and anonymous male figure in his poem *Farmhand*. Like Bhatt and Wordsworth, Baxter presents a single, solitary figure who we take to be emblematic. In Baxter's case this type is an agricultural labourer, at ease at work and with other men, but feeling awkward and out-of-place among women. As the title makes clear, he's a man defined as much by his work as by his gender, as if almost his whole sense of self has been subsumed by his line of work, and in his case his usefulness on a farm. Like the other two poets, Baxter honours an obscure, marginalised and probably impoverished character, revealing the sensitivity, loneliness and the humanity buried beneath a rough and ruddy exterior.

Like the other poets, Baxter also keeps his style plain, immediately intelligible and conversational, like a working man speaking to working men, with just the odd dash of figurative imagery. Like Bhatt and unlike Wordsworth, he eschews regular metre. Unlike Bhatt and like Wordsworth, he arranges the lines into regular, neatly constructed stanzas. Obviously, in contrast to the other two poets, Baxter describes a male character and his theme, in part, is maleness. There's something winning, I think, in the fact that this poet doesn't bring himself into the poem and make himself its subject, at least not explicitly. Baxter doesn't invite us to admire his poetic soul. There's a gentleness to the poem too, created by the unhurried descriptions, the steadily composed stanzas, the poet's empathetic attention and by the unobtrusive use of half-rhymes.

---

[5] See Hamilton & Noel-Todd, *Oxford Companion to Modern Poetry*, pp. 34-35.

Indeed, reading the poem through the first time you might not have noticed the rhymes, even though they are positioned conventionally at the end of each line. Baxter employs a consistent, unchanging envelope rhyme scheme, so that the first line of each quatrain rhymes with the fourth line and the two internal lines chime with each other. This seems an appropriate scheme, for a contemplative and introspective poem. It's a good fit too for the farmhand's life of routine and repetition. Most of the rhymes are half-rhymes, such as the deft 'cigarette' & 'secret night'; 'flowers' & 'that tears'; 'watch him' & 'engine'. Only three pairs, 'through' & 'to', 'making' & 'breaking' and 'strong' & 'song' are full, with the last of these creating a little sonic harmony, echoing the idea of song. The short pause indicated by the hyphen after 'strong' also gives the word a little extra sonic push. Mostly Baxter uses enjambment, so that sentences run over the ends of lines and into each other, further tucking in and dampening down the sonic effects. There's a quiet artistry at work here, going about its craft without drawing a lot of attention to itself. In other words, the poet's style - modest, understated, avoiding linguistic fancy-danness - parallels the farmhand's character. Clearly, in many ways Baxter identifies with this man.

Drifting like flowers

The farmhand is an outsider at the dancehall. He hovers, symbolically, at the door, as if awkwardly unsure whether to enter or withdraw, at the threshold of a world of which he doesn't feel part, but nevertheless he's attracted to. He's also positioned with 'his back/ against the wall' which could suggest casualness, but also defensiveness and ill-ease. To him, it seems the world of the dancehall is rather mysterious – he looks 'out into the secret night' as if serving for answers in the darkness. Of course, the main thing he lacks is a partner and he cannot help watching the girls. Like Wordsworth, Baxter compares women to flowers, but here the simile implies they seem delicate and beautiful, but also alien to the farmhand, with their 'drifting' movements unpredictable as a stream or a breeze. Their unfamiliarity to him is also indicated by the way they are undifferentiated as 'girls'. The close-up focus on his 'sunburnt face' and 'hairy hands' signals that the farmhand is not refined and suggests that he feels clumsy and self-conscious in the presence of these attractive young women.

Not made for dancing

Baxter uses a series of straightforward contrasts to convey how the farmhand feels and what he does and doesn't have: He feels out-of-place and inadequate at the dance hall, for instance, but he is well suited for agricultural labour; he doesn't have a girl, but has his

hopes and dreams instead. The farmhand's capacity for finer feelings is conveyed through the emotive effect music has on him. Mostly, Baxter stays on the surface in his descriptions, as if observing the man from the outside. However, in this crucial instance, like an omniscient narrator in a novel, he allows us into the character's thoughts and emotions. The music has a visceral, almost physical impact on the farmhand, it 'tears' 'an old wound open', either suggesting the man has felt like this before, or perhaps that he has loved and lost a woman in the past. In either case, the imagery indicates sensitivity and emotional suffering.

What is the effect of the odd little word, the exclamation 'ah', in the first line of the last stanza? What tone does it convey? Surprise? Pleasure? To me, it signals admiration, as the poet invites us to see the farmhand in his natural environment. From a narrative perspective, it's the equivalent of an intrusive narrator, stepping into a story to make sure the reader forms a particular attitude to a character. The sonic physicality in the succeeding line, with its fuller, rounder sounds, is almost muscular; '*For*king **st**ooks, ef*for*tless and **st**rong', with the 'for' sounds combining with 'st', 'k' and 'ing' and 'ong' and a bunching of stressed syllables. This contrasts sonically with the next line. Here an alliterative run of gentle 'l's complements the loosening of stresses, appropriate for the subject of love and song. The sound of the tractor engine is like music to the farmhand's ears, perfect and clear, again indicating that he has the capacity to appreciate beauty. Plus this music doesn't open up painful wounds.

We see the farmhand through the poet's sympathetic, but not sentimental gaze, and hear of him through the poet's unaffected, straight-speaking voice. Mostly the poem is constructed on contrasts, but the most important relationship, between poet, poem and subject is one of similarity and harmony. Seeing himself as a figure of the 'wilderness' the poet identifies and empathises with the farmhand and encourages us to do so too. Baxter has written a poem that is both a portrait and a mirror: a sketch of the farmhand and, reflected within it, an image of the poet himself.

Farmhand crushed:

SEE – DOOR – WALL – SECRET – ALWAYS – GIRLS – MUSIC – WOUND – SUNBURNT – LOVE-MAKING – EARTH – PLOUGH – GIRL – GIGGLE – COUPLES – ENVIOUS – AH – EFFORTLESS – LOVER – TRACTOR.

Isobel Dixon, *Plenty*

Weather Eye

Born and brought-up in the semi-desert Karoo region of South Africa, Isobel Dixon moved to Scotland as a post graduate student and now lives in England where she works as a literary agent. According to the British Council's Literature website, Dixon's 'poetry represents her personal experiences in often unforgiving landscapes'[6], a description that certainly applies to the seemingly autobiographical poem *Plenty*.

The poem is structured upon a stark contrast, between a there-and-then and a here-and-now. The 'there' is the house where the poet grew up and the harsh landscape of 'drought' around it. The 'then' is the 'lean, dry times' of her childhood. The 'here' and 'now' are not specified, but this second temporal and spatial location is 'plentiful' and comfortable - the opposite to the hard-pressed, perhaps impoverished, 'there' and 'then' of the past. Hence it may seem, superficially at least, that the latter is superior to the former, and that the poem presents a positive movement from a hard, difficult past to a brighter, more comfortable present. However, this binary is undercut by the nostalgic affection with which the poet recalls the past and by the feelings of sadness at her current separation from her sisters and her mother. Perhaps, too, referring to herself as a lover of luxury [a 'sybarite'] and to the shower's plenty as 'excess, almost' suggests she feels some guilt about her current comfort. That off-hand hedge, 'almost', is as big a clue as any

---

[6] https://literature.britishcouncil.org/writer/isobel-dixon

to the poet's fundamental mixed feelings.

The poem is dominated by four figures - the tub and the shower, the narrator and her mother. The first two of these are metonyms, parts standing in for the whole. The significance of the tub is indicated by the detailed attention lavished on it: A stanza's worth of lines informs us that it was an 'old enamel tub', that it was 'age-stained' and also 'pocked', that it had 'griffin claws' for legs and 'fat brass taps' [note the attention-attracting, sonically thickening assonance] and, most significantly, that it was 'never full'. For a poem characterised by a lean, spare style and thrifty use of adjectives, that's an awful lot of description for an inanimate object. Moreover, the tub is made significant through personification, a feature particularly noticeable, as Dixon uses figurative imagery as sparely as she deploys adjectives. On top of this, the tub is on the children's side, it was their 'old compliant co-conspirator' in the battle against her mother's austerity, a conspirator that delivered something 'lovely'.

An impression is given that there was something especially pleasurable about sneaking 'another precious inch' of warm water from the only 'fat' thing around, and in going against her mother's stern restrictions. For one thing, Dixon tells us that this experience was the 'best of all' and describes it as a 'lovely sin'. In addition, the language grows more lyrical at this point in the poem, with an alliterative run of liquidy 'l's flowing through 'lovely', 'lolling' and 'luxuriant', sensual reference to 'secret warmth' and assonance and internal rhyme combining in those 'fat brass taps'. In contrast, although it produces a 'hot cascade', the modern shower receives little attention, suggesting that the poet feels far less affection for it.

A clasp to keep us all from chaos

The semantic dissonance of the phrase 'lovely sin' is another example of the poet's ambivalence. The same ambivalence can be traced in the description of the mother and her daughter and of the relationship between them. It stems from the different perspectives of the narrator as a child at the time, and now, as an adult, looking back. The mother is presented as being characteristically unsmiling and angry, specifically, so the narrator thinks, at her. In addition, her children 'thought her mean' and ineffectual [they run 'riot', 'skipped chores' and rebel against their mother's prohibitions, albeit secretly]. On the other hand, the phrase 'quiet despair' generates great sympathy for the mother, emphasising the difficulty she faced in keeping house and home together, seemingly as the only parent of five unruly children.

Dixon uses figurative imagery especially effectively to express her mixed feelings about her mother. The reference, for instance, to her 'Mommy's smile' suggests affection, not least through the childish intimacy of 'mommy', in comparison to her previous more formal reference to 'my mother'. However, this promised smile is said to have 'stalled', like the landscape's windmills. By comparing her warmest, most human expression to something mechanical, the description rather dehumanises the mother. Similarly, the description of her mouth 'anchored down' creates sympathy, in that the mother is clearly burdened by her responsibilities and unhappy, but, on the other hand,

 again compares her to something inanimate and suggests a rather relentless, unchanging irascibility with her young daughter. The poet seems almost fixated with her mother's mouth – there are no references to her eyes or her face, to her hands or her touch – and in both descriptions the metonymic mouth is compared to inanimate objects – a 'clasp' and a 'lid' that 'clamped hard'.

Both images, of course, convey the mother's efforts to hold things together and the terrible strain of this on her character. Clasps and clamps keep things together - to 'clasp' suggests a degree of desperation and 'clamp' implies considerable force, re-enforced by the

adjective 'hard'. A 'lid' is designed, obviously, to contain things. On the one hand, these images create sympathy as they communicate how hard the mother had to work and how joyless the experience was for her. But on the other hand, as with the sail image, they dehumanise her, particularly as the images are associated with her mouth, potentially a source of smiles and words and, potentially, the communication of motherly love. Words, naturally, are also very precious things for poets.

In the final stanza, Dixon returns to the image of her mother's mouth which she now 'misses'. Like the mother, the mouth has been liberated. 'Loosed from the bonds' of bringing up children in such trying circumstances, it is now fully a 'smile'. Conveying a sense of release, this image is, of course, the opposite to the early ones of anchors, clasps, lids and clamps. That  small phrase 'at last' is highly significant. It suggests that, though she may have wanted to before, it has taken the poet a long time for her to come to appreciate her mother's love - as in at last she has come to miss her mother's smile. But it also implies that perhaps it has also taken the mother a long time to unclasp and de-clamp herself, to recover and let go of the past, so that she can now truly express her affection for her daughter at last. Emotionally, of course, 'at last' also adds to the sense of release and relief.

Perhaps the poem's form also embodies Dixon's ambivalent feelings. On the one hand [a phrase we've used a lot about this poem] all the stanzas are arranged in neat, consistent, orderly quatrains, with lines in each stanza of a similar length. But on the other hand, the line lengths vary considerably between stanzas and there's no governing metre or rhyme scheme to keep everything under strict control. In this way, perhaps, the poem's form reflects the poet's mother's attempts to impose order on 'chaos'. Moreover, it seems that the poet may have inherited this orderliness, in an artistic sense at least. That said, within and against that outer orderliness roaming freely is the poet's still rebellious, unruly childhood spirit.

Plenty crunched:

FIVE – RIOT – TUB – NEVER – DROUGHT – DRY – SMILE – ANCHORED – MINE – CLASP – LOCKS – SPILLING – BREAD – TOO – LID – MEAN – BEST – EARSHOT – STOLE – LOVELY – SECRET – FAT – CO-CONSPIRATORS – SYBARITE – CASCADE – EXCESS – I – MISS – LAST – SMILE – CHILDHOOD.

Robert Hayden, *Those Winter Sundays*

Heart-shape in the dust

Though he was a black American poet writing in the twentieth century, the language of Hayden's unconventional-looking sonnet makes the poem sound like ordinary colloquial English speech. Hayden employs Standard English and uses diction comprised of ordinary, everyday words, and these the poet arranges in familiar syntactical patterns – hence the poem presents few problems of interpretation for readers. Whereas more overtly political contemporaries challenged White English and the dominance of white culture, particularly by writing in non-standard English, Hayden's poem presents his relationship with his father in universalized and universalising terms.

In *Those Winter Sundays*, Hayden eschews regular metre and rhyme and uses figurative imagery only very sparingly, so that, overall, the language of the poem is down-to-earth, straightforward and prosaic. Take, for example, the first sentence: In the opening lines the poet creates the impression that readers are joining a conversation or monologue that has already started beforehand: 'Sundays **too** my father got up early'. We are being addressed here almost as if we are the poets' friends. The verbs in this sentence are the most basic monosyllables – 'got', 'put', 'made' – and the clauses are linked as simply as is possible, through 'and' and 'then'. Hence the intimate, conversational style is quickly established. However, towards the end of this first sentence the language becomes heightened a little through a combination of small-scale poetic devices: Synaesthesia turns something tactile ['cold'] into something visual ['blueblack']; a metonym is used, whereby the father's 'cracked hands' stand in for the wider damage of years of hard labour; sonically there's a double pattern of assonance, with short and long 'a' sounds weaving through 'cracked' - 'hand' – 'banked' and 'ached' – 'labor' – 'day' – 'made' – 'blaze'. Patches of alliteration ['weekday weather'; 'banked' 'blaze'] and internal rhyme ['labor'; 'weather'] also help thicken the opening sentence's sonic texture.

The more self-consciously worked and poetic language is used when describing the father tending the fire. The following line drops back into conversational idiom - a contrast that accentuates the bluntness of the sentiment. This bluntness is emphasised by the use of a sentence fragment finishing with a full stop: 'No one ever thanked him.'. Though it is constructed from ordinary, conversational language, at times, Hayden gives his poem a more lyrical ring. The style is best illustrated by the poem's regretful and resonant final lines.

Though the words forming the question are simple, common monosyllables, repetition of the rhetorical device lends the penultimate line a distinctly plaintive tone, 'What did I know? What did I know?'. The key plaintive 'o' sound is carried into the next line, echoing in 'lonely'. Other delicate sonic effects enrich the lines, particularly the alliteration of 'love's' and 'lonely', the assonance of 'austere' and 'offices' and the sibilant run of 's sounds through 'love's', 'austere' and 'offices'. In addition, characteristically, the poet combines seemingly unpoetic, matter-of-fact vocabulary - most obviously 'offices' – with that most romantic, poetic of words, 'love'. We might also think of 'austerity' as an opposite of 'love'; the former concerns lack and restriction, whereas the latter involves generosity and giving. Hence

Hayden's combination of words that do not normally appear in close relation makes the idea of 'love's austere and lonely offices' surprising and striking. Furthermore, 'lonely' might also make us notice the absence of a wife/mother figure in the poem, an absence that adds further poignancy and may lie behind the reference to 'chronic angers'. Hence the technique of the poem underlines the poet's point; that as a boy he did not recognise the love expressed through his father's quiet actions. Only as an adult, does he come to this realisation, perhaps too late to thank his father in person, but not too late to honour his memory in this verse.

The cold

The adjective 'cold' is repeated three times in this short poem. Its importance is also emphasised by the word's appearance at the ends of lines, through its presence in each stanza and via the double use of synaesthesia. Obviously, the poet is referring to literal and metaphorical coldness, and it is his father who 'drives' this out. Coldness seems to have been the natural atmosphere of the poet's childhood home and he himself appears to have been 'cold' to his father, 'speaking indifferently to him' and neglecting to thank him. The sad poignancy of the poem is generated by the contrast between the indifference and lack of appreciation the poet felt as a child and his awareness now of the unostentatious, selfless love that his father's actions expressed.

If it wasn't apparent to the boy that his father's actions expressed love, it's also not obvious to the reader that Hayden's poem is, in fact, a sonnet, a form especially associated with love. There's no octave or sestet or volta. The lines do not run in pentameter and there's no familiar sonnet rhyme scheme of either the Petrarchan or Shakespearian variety. Often Petrarchan and Shakespearian sonnets express intense feelings for a lover, male or female. Hayden uses the form to express a different, quieter kind of love and he re-engineers the sonnet form accordingly, dampening down its most showy features.

This then is a sonnet, but not as we know it. Simple actions expressed his father's love, though the boy did not know it at the time. Hence, understated, unpretentious and down-to-earth, Hayden's poem matches form and style to subject and in doing so expresses strong feelings with memorable economy.

Those Winter Sundays crunched:

TOO – COLD – ACHED – LABOR – BLAZE – BREAKING – WARM – SLOWLY – FEARING – INDIFFERENTLY – DRIVEN – POLISHED – KNOW – LOVE'S.

Seamus Heaney, *Mid-Term Break*

Revealing this poem's narrative one stanza at a time will help build-up the readers' expectations and should ensure that the final lines have their intended emotional impact. [Even if you've already read the

poem before, doing your own version of this exercise will still help highlight how the narrative develops.] So, if you're a teacher, show your class just the first stanza and give your students a few minutes, working in pairs, to discuss and then write down what they think might be happening in the poem.

Sophisticated students could be encouraged to also consider stylistic and structural elements of the poem, such as its conversational language and tercet stanza form. The following is an example of my own thinking as the poem reveals itself:

No gaudy scars

The first stanza appears to be straightforward enough. The narrator recounts a day when he was at college and, for some as yet unstated reason, he had to return home. Though he could be facing some form of disciplinary punishment, we might assume that he was unwell, as he's in the 'sick bay'. We might also infer that the college is a school rather than university as there are 'bells' signalling lesson time, and thus that the narrator is, therefore, recounting an incident from his childhood. Perhaps we might also wonder why the 'neighbours' rather than his parent pick the boy up. Perhaps too we might wonder what the delay might signal – why does he have to wait 'all morning' to be picked up from school? The tone seems quite neutral, almost matter-of-fact. Nothing too alarming seems to be taking place.

It's a bit of a shock then, I think, the first line of the second stanza. As it must have been for the boy who'd rarely seen his father crying before. So, this makes us speculate about what terrible event could have upset the father so much. The word 'funeral' makes us immediately wonder if, perhaps, someone has died. The last line confirms that something awful has happened, but doesn't reveal what exactly; 'it was a hard blow'. [Retrospectively, of course Big Jim's words are horribly clumsy, yet also horribly apt, with their inadvertently brutal accuracy.] So, now we can be pretty sure that the boy has been collected by the neighbours because his father wasn't in a fit state to do so and that he's returned from school not because he had done something wrong or because he was ill, but because of some event that has happened while he was away from home.

The first line of the next stanza comes as a relief. The tone changes with the baby's happy gurgling at the sight of its big brother. Why are the men standing up to shake the narrator's hand though? Usually this is a sign of congratulation or celebration. Perhaps the boy has achieved some notable success at school. We might also wonder why these old men are gathered in the boy's house. By this time, too, we may be beginning to worry about where the boy's mother might be. Alarm bells might be starting to ring in some readers' minds.

Structurally this third stanza is a little different to the previous two. The first ends with a full stop after 'home' and we infer a considerable space of time has elapsed before the second stanza begins. The second stanza also ends with a full-stop, allowing the phrase 'hard blow' to resonate in the reader's mind. Each of these two stanzas seem complete, solid units of meaning. In contrast, the third tercet is incomplete with the last line enjambed over and into the following stanza. There's a subtle sense of intensification and concentration, a quickening up and a slight loosening of control.

By the start of the fourth stanza any thoughts that the boy might be being congratulated can be dismissed. But still we don't know the cause of the odd behaviour. 'Sorry for my trouble' sounds like another euphemism; like a 'hard blow' it could cover a very broad range of experiences, from the fairly trivial to the most serious. Like 'hard blow' it sounds like the sort of thing people say when they don't know what else to say. Why are the people whispering? Usually this is a sign of respect, or mourning. 'Away at school', coupled with the drive home, suggests that the boy no longer lived at home, so the fact that he has been fetched back must be the more significant. With relief we come across the reference to his 'mother'. As with the previous stanza the fourth ends with the word 'hand'. Perhaps touch is a form of intimate communication we reach for when words fail. What kind of a poem is this? It seemed like a poem about a childhood memory, perhaps about growing-up. Now we might begin to guess that actually it's an elegy. A sense of dread builds up in the reader.

The last line of stanza four runs on into the opening of the fifth. Whereas the timeframe and location shifts in the opening stanzas, these succeeding ones concentrate our attention in the domestic interior and a particular moment. Time seems to both slow down [Heaney describes several small actions in detail] and paradoxically speed up [the stanzas run in to each other without pause]. Why would the mother be 'angry'? Angry about what? Against whom? An ambulance arrives, so maybe a member of the family has been taken seriously ill? A grandparent perhaps. That fleeting hope that someone is ill and not dead is immediately crushed in the next line - the fears circulating our reading for a while now, like those that must have been going through the head of the young boy, land like a blow with the categorically unequivocal words 'the corpse'. Would it have made any difference if Heaney had used a gentler synonym? Something less cold and harsh and clinical, such as 'body'? Of course it would; that's the point.

'Stanched and bandaged'. Why? What do these two words suggest? Can we link them back now to a 'hard blow'? What do we think may have happened? 'Stanch' or 'staunch' means to stop blood flowing, usually from a wound. If a grandparent had died in their sleep, for example, why would they be brought to their son or daughter's house in an 'ambulance' and why would their body be 'stanched and bandaged'? Clearly then, sickeningly, the tragedy unfolding before us doesn't just concern a death but also the manner of that death.

There is a time shift again in stanza six. We jump forward to the 'next morning'. It is as if there was nothing else to say, no words, after the corpse was brought in. Still, Heaney continues to withhold from us the identity of the dead person. By now, we're pretty sure it must be a

relative and a close one at that. The devastating grief the boy must have felt remains unexpressed as he, and perhaps the author remembering this event, concentrate on the hard facts of the matter – 'next morning I went up into the room' – is entirely factual and emotionally colourless, almost numb. References to 'snowdrops' and 'candles' are poignant. Signs of mourning and remembrance, they also symbolically attempt to 'soothe' the 'bedside' in lieu of being able to 'soothe' anything or anyone else. We now learn the dead person is male.

The poem's extraordinary emotional restraint continues into the delicate and intimate penultimate stanza. The verb 'wearing' suggests for a moment that the wound might be superficial, that it could be taken off like a piece of clothing. This implies that the boy narrator cannot fully understand death nor take in the fact that this person is really dead. Though it is straightforwardly factual, the second line lands like a blow. Perhaps we have suspected that the dead person was a younger sibling, after all Heaney was the 'eldest', but we probably hoped this wasn't the case. The size of the box, just 'four-foot' tells us the dead person was a very young child, just a toddler. Any doubt we might have had about their tender age is removed by the word 'cot' rather than 'bed'. And finally, we're told, that this small, young lad has been killed in a road accident, hit by a car: 'the bumper knocked him clear.'

Note the awful finality of that last piece of punctuation.

Depending on your own or your class's emotional response to the poem, you can decide whether to reveal the final line now, or whether to withhold it for a little while longer. If you/ they can bear it, ask them to try to compose the last stanza of the poem. Give them only a few minutes to discuss with a partner what they would write and then make them write down a few lines each. When they've all written at least a line or two, reveal the poem's final, single line stanza and discuss its force.

The last line repeats the key devastating information about the size of the box and then confirms what the reader probably has guessed already and dreads to hear, that the dead child was very young, only four years old. Isolating this line and leaving only space after it, adds to its devastating impact. The combination of the stark single line and the only full rhyme in the poem ensure that it hits home and lingers long in the reader's mind. Adding anything after the last full stop would have detracted from the impact.

Less is more?

Although Heaney describes his father and mother's emotions through their crying and tears, he doesn't say anything explicitly either about his own feelings at the time or as an adult looking back on this family tragedy. What might this suggest about his feelings? That he didn't and doesn't have any? That would make him a monster. That the experience made him feel numb? Considering the lack of explicit reference to the narrator's emotions, how does Heaney manage to make the poem so emotionally powerful? Consider the alternatives. A different sort of poet, perhaps an American or Southern European one, for instance, might have written a howling rage of a poem about such a traumatic experience, a sonic blast expressing their raging feelings. Or imagine Heaney's poem as part of a Hollywood blockbuster, *The Poet*. Typically a Hollywood director would try to ring every last drop of unhappy emotion out of this sort of scene – mawkish lingering close-ups of sad faces, tears in slow-mo soft focus, lachrymose soundtrack, the whole hysterical works. In contrast, Heaney's elegiac poem is emotionally and stylistically spare, understated, reserved. The emotions are held, kept in check by ordinary, conversational, matter-of-fact language arranged in orderly fashion. For me, this style actually makes the poem far more powerful than it would be if all the emotion was splashed about. Heaney takes us into the scene and we, the readers, makes us anticipate the end, builds up a sense of dread, and makes us imagine the feelings swirling like dark water under the seemingly calm and collected words. This engages us, involves us emotionally in the story as it develops. And it doesn't take much imagination to imagine grief and mourning. This way, too, we see how Heaney as a boy, and later as a man, struggled to know how to react, to properly process the horror of what had happened. The poem embodies a struggle to control intense feelings, to be brave and hold things together. The style is also true to the culture in which Heaney lived and the way people spoke. Elsewhere in his poetry, for instance, the poet refers to a pervasive cultural reserve and tight-lippedness. Finally, another reason for the restrained style is that Heaney isn't an egocentric or self-pitying writer; he doesn't want the main focus of the poem to be drawn to his own suffering.

Looking at the poem as a whole, we may wonder at Heaney's choice of metrical and stanzaic form. *Mid-Term Break* is written in pentameter, but only rarely does this regularise into even and predictable lines of iambic pattern. Though there are five beats in most of the lines, the iambic pattern is often distorted and disrupted, subtly signalling the tensions under the calm surface. Pentameter in poetry is traditionally a form used for serious subjects. Heaney may have chosen the tercet form to reflect the three principle characters – himself, his parents and his little brother. The fact that it's unrhymed suits the unshowy, down-to-earth, low key style of the poem. Surely it would have been a betrayal of the truth of the experience and of his brother's death if Heaney had written a poem that drew attention to its own style through spectacular metaphors, diction or rhyming. Though, the poem comes from his first, mainly autobiographical collection, *Death of a Naturalist*, published in 1966, Heaney doesn't want his writing skill to be the main focus of our attention.

Poignantly the ghost spirit of the poet's little brother appears from time to time throughout the almost half a century of poetry that followed *Death of a Naturalist*. Sometimes he hovers in the background or just beyond the frame of a poem or is alluded to indirectly through metaphor or symbolism. At other times the lost child moves more into the poem's foreground. In *The Blackbird of Glanmore*, for instance, written forty years after *Mid-Term Break*, Heaney makes explicit his association of blackbirds and love for them with his 'lost brother', who he calls a 'little stillness dancer', a dancer he finds still 'cavorting through the yard,/ So glad to see me home'.

Mid-Term Break crunched:

MORNING – BELLS – NEIGHBOURS – CRYING – FUNERALS – BLOW – BABY – EMBARRASSED – HAND – TROUBLE – WHISPERS – MOTHER – ANGRY – AMBULANCE – CORPSE – SNOWDROPS – SOOTHED – PALER – BRUISE – FOUR-FOOT – BUMPER – YEAR.

Stevie Smith, *Not Waving But Drowning*

Not waving or drowning

What do you make of the illustration above? What does it illustrate exactly? It's the sketch Smith produced to go alongside this poem. To me, though the body is androgynous, it looks like the figure is probably female – narrow face, big eyes, long straight, perhaps rather bedraggled, hair. The figure also appears to be standing upright quite easily, in slightly choppy, wavy water that is barely waist-deep. Their expression is composed and regards us calmly enough, with a hint of a smile perhaps. And their body looks relaxed and static, with their arms down by their sides and hands submerged, perhaps leaning a little out towards us.

My point is that this figure doesn't look much like the main character in Smith's poem: It's not male; it doesn't look like it is speaking or moaning; it's not flailing in a way that could be interpreted as either waving or drowning; it doesn't appear to be any danger or distress. The incongruous picture adds an extra knotty, difficult to reconcile tension to a comic/ sad poem composed of a series of seemingly irresolvable tensions.

 Smith's poem would lend itself productively to a cloze exercise. This exercise will help students notice the surreal aspects of the poem, particularly the mixture of tones and idioms, the combination of a cheery chatty colloquial voice with a matter-of-fact narrator and a mournfully dead speaker.

Nobody heard him, the ………. man,
But still he lay moaning:
I was much …………… than you thought
And not waving but ……………..

Poor chap, he always loved …………
And now he's …………
It must have been too cold for him his heart gave way,
They said.

Oh, no ……………., it was too cold always
(Still the …….. one lay moaning)
I was much ………… all my life
And not waving but …………..

In *The Cambridge Introduction to English Poetry, 1945-2010*, Eric Falci opines that 'Smith's endemic playfulness is of a sardonic and often disturbing sort' and identifies a mismatch between form and subject as a key characteristic of her poetry; 'her lyrics use the jauntiness of form to cover a darkness of substance'[7]. With this in mind, it's not surprising that critics can't seem to quite decide what to make of Smith's work. Is it serious, profound poetry presented in light comic form? Or is it just light and comical, even rather silly stuff masquerading as profundity? Is Smith's work innocent, naïve and childlike [i.e. good art], or is it childish, arch or flippant [i.e. bad art]? Is she an absurdist, a satirist or

---

[7] *The Cambridge Introduction to British Poetry*, pp. 30-33.

perhaps even a surrealist? Nobody seems to be sure.

Mad hatter logic

The major reason for the uncertainty, it seems, is Smith's bravura throwing together of tragic and comic elements in her poetry and the consequently disorientating tonal shifts. Plus there's a weird internal logic of poems that don't resolve into any coherent sense. Take *Not Waving But Drowning*: In the first line we are informed that 'nobody' could hear the 'dead man'. That doesn't really make sense. For one thing, if the man is entirely deceased then he wouldn't be making any noise, to be heard or unheard. Perhaps the second line will clarify things? Fat chance. Now we learn that the dead man lay 'moaning'. Surely by definition if you're dead you can't make any noise at all, not even moaning. And what are we to make of the adjective 'still'? Is he stationary, as we might expect of a corpse, or does he continue to moan? Not sure. In any case, the bystanders [perhaps friends?] are not able to hear the moans coming from the dead man. We, it seems, can, however, as in the third line the narrative perspective shifts from an anonymous third person narrator to first person and we hear the dead man speaking. But are these words spoken, or are we to suppose we are being given access to the avowedly dead man's thoughts? The lack of speech marks leaves this issue unresolved. If we aren't disorientated enough already, the second stanza starts with what sounds like dialogue, 'poor chap…'. Clearly, we've switched out of the dead man's perspective and into another third person perspective. But is this the same perspective as that in the first stanza? No – at the end of the stanza we learn that this speaker is one of the 'they' that cannot hear the dead man, as opposed to the narrator and readers who can. Oddly, but perhaps predictably enough, as well as still being able to make sounds and engage in cerebral processes, the corpse appears to be able to hear the other people who can't hear him. In the third stanza the dead man contradicts the previous speaker's, or speakers', account of how he died. It's hard to escape the sense that the poet is playing some sort of whimsically eccentric game with, or perhaps, on the reader.

Evidently, this poem can't be deciphered using rational thinking and logic – it doesn't operate in that way. Tonally, also it's hard to interpret. There are three main tones, each expressed by one of the speakers. The narrator's tone sounds initially to be factual and neutral, merely documenting what's happening. On closer inspection, there's a hint of something else, perhaps impatience in the use of 'still' and the bracketed interjection in the last stanza ['still the dead one lay moaning']. Add to that Smith's use of the word 'moaning'. If the poet had just wanted the sense of pain, she could have used 'groaning' just as easily. 'Moaning', however, carries the sense of whingeing or

complaining, which means making a fuss about something insignificant, which hardly seems to apply to dying. Hence the narrator's tone seems rather inappropriate: 'Stop moaning about being dead, will you please?' The dead man's tone is more obviously emotional, perhaps plaintive or even angry, particularly at the start of the last stanza, 'oh, no no no...' This tone clashes strikingly with the almost jaunty third speaker: 'Poor chap, he always loved larking'. That really doesn't seem the right emotional response to discovering someone has died does it. This speaker doesn't sound terribly distressed at all. There's something quite casual, almost off-hand about the words from this oddly pluralized, anonymous 'they'.

If we step back a little from the perspective of the speakers to that of the writer another tone comes into earshot. Running behind or underneath the sprightly tone of the bystander, making the poem's music more complex, is a darker tone. Sardonic would be a good way to describe it. A dark, grim almost gallows style humour is at play here, exposing the inappropriate and inadequate response to death by the bystanders.

Whimsical and sprightly
If there's a metrical pattern, it is as hard to decipher as anything else in the poem. Arguably the first stanza follows loosely a hymn or ballad metre of alternating lines of tetrameter and trimeter:

'No**body heard** him, the **dead man**
But **still** he **lay moan**ing
I was **much furth**er **out** than you **thought**
And **not wav**ing but **drown**ing'

Even if we accept this scansion, the stresses still fall higgledy-piggledy, with no discernible or predictable pattern to the iambs and trochees. Moreover, by the second stanza the whole arrangement has skewed alarmingly out of kilter. In particular, the second line is far too short [though this adds to the bluntness of the sentiment] and the third line is far, far too long, containing twelve monosyllables and perhaps six stresses. And the fourth is even shorter than the second, with just two words and only two measly syllables ['they said']. Try scanning the first line of the final stanza. Go on. Exactly. We can be fairly certain that '**cold** always' take stress, but the metre of 'oh, no no no, it was too...' could be interpreted in any number of ways.

So, what are we to make of it all, this poem that veers alarmingly between undifferentiated but different speakers and a variety of inappropriate tones, a poem that metrically is so scrambled and erratic and that has a narrative that won't resolve into any sort of logical sense? How can we unpick its knotted tensions? To me, reading Smith's poem is the literary equivalent of looking at an Escher painting, such as the one on the next page, called *Convex and Concave* [1955]. *Not Waving But Drowning*'s a sort of linguistic illusion or puzzle, hinting at, but seeming to deny, the possibility of full resolution. The poem seems to invite lines of interpretation, only to make the reader run up impossible cul-de-sacs and end up lost down dead ends. That said, perhaps applying reasoned analysis to this poem isn't the way to unlock an interpretation.

Come, Death, and carry me away

Smith was fond of paradox and, according to Anthony Thwaite, as the poet got older the 'theme of death' 'increasingly preoccupied her'[8].

---

[8] *Oxford Companion to Modern Literature*, p. 573.

Almost paradoxically, she tended to present death in a 'whimsical and even sprightly way', sometimes even as 'someone to be comfortably welcomed', according to the same critic. So, my reading of this poem is

that the narrator, a version of Smith, is so intimate and closely in touch with death that, like a medium, she can actually hear from the 'other side', such as this particular dead man. This is a 'talent' or almost supernatural sensitivity or peculiarly acute power of empathy that ordinary people lack; hence the bystanders cannot hear the dead. There is a tension in the narrator's feelings as she is ambivalent about being so attuned to death.

Perhaps she cannot block it out and the communication only seems to go one way; hence the hint of impatience in their lines. The super-sensitive narrator/ Smith is also especially able to hear the voices of people who have suffered lives of quiet despair, because she herself had felt this quiet despair and has, indeed, almost courted death in her poetry. This dead man could have called for help and seems to have accepted his own death with equanimity. In fact, the poem hints that he may even have committed suicide. Part of the poet identifies with despair, but another part can also, to some extent, resist and distance herself from such overwhelming feelings. This, then, is the poem's central knotty and unresolved tension, the tension between the pull towards and the pull against death.

Drowning, not waving

The fact that onlookers presumed the dead man was 'waving' when he was, in fact, drowning powerfully conveys the difficulty we all have in understanding other people's interior worlds, particularly other people's psychological suffering. We can only read each other from the outside and even then we are prone, like these bystanders, to completely misinterpret what we see. Appearances are often deceptive and our perceptions fallible. The onlookers speak as one, as a 'they', because they present the general view. From the outside, and from a distance, the man looked to be absolutely fine, perfectly happy. When, in fact, as the poet instinctively knew, he always felt 'too far out' and 'too cold'.

Smith's poem seems to me to be an utterly brilliant one. There's a leanness, an economy of style which means not a word is unnecessary. It has an immediate emotive impact, but also lingers long in the memory. It's simple, but also complex, playful, but also serious. We all, feel sometimes and at various times like one of its characters – misunderstood and suffering, disconnected and not bothered, disturbed by our empathy for other people's suffering. Like Gothic literature it also radically destabilises and overturns one of the most fundamental binaries by which we conceptualise our experiences, that between life and death. And also it retains its mystery, continuing to escape complete rational interpretation.

Not Waving But Drowning squeezed:

DEAD – MOANING – MUCH – DROWNING – CHAP – DEAD – COLD – THEY – NO – STILL – ALL – DROWNING.

Rosemary Dobson, *The Three Fates*

Who wants to live forever?

Dreams of immortality have haunted the human imagination for as long as humans have had imaginations. Heaven/ Nirvana/ Valhalla/ the Elysian fields all offer enticing visions of life eternal. But alongside and underneath those dreams have lurked fears of immortality, most obviously embodied in Christian thought by the endless torments of hell, but also in visions of human beings endlessly old, but unable to die, doomed to drag their decaying bodies across the earth for all eternity. The history of literature is also full of stories of tragically lost loves, star-crossed lovers and of the extremes lovers will go to try to be re-united, even after death. Dobson's poem, for instance, might make us think of *Orpheus and Eurydice* among other stories of such doomed romance.

Dobson's poem portrays a man tempted in the direst of extremis to wish for 'Life everlasting', only to find himself caught in a repeated loop and re-living the same life over and, the poem implies, over again. Rather than being able to change the pattern that led him so close to being drowned - perhaps, the poems hints, a suicide attempt driven by grief - the poem's protagonist is stuck watching his own life running backwards before there is 'an instant's pause' and time moves forward again. The man is presented as being helpless, almost becoming a spectator of his own existence and, in a filmic poem, in which each stanza captures a scene in the narrative, Dobson's use of the metaphor of the film 'reel unrolling' confirms that this story is as fixed and unalterable as fate. Do what he might, this man will arrive at no other place than the 'river' in which he will nearly drown.

 The strong narrative thread of the poem and its reverse chronology makes it an excellent candidate for an unscrambling exercise. In this instance, just scramble the order of the lines, erase the stanza breaks and see if the class can arrive at the correct form and sequence. If they get stuck and you're feeling kind, give them the first and last lines. This exercise will have the benefit of allowing pupils to discover the poem's reverse chronology for themselves.

The reel unrolling

According to *The Oxford Companion to Modern Poetry*, the 'chief occupation' in the work of one of Australia's foremost poets, Rosemary Dobson [1920-2012] is time. Dobson is also celebrated for a long poetic career that lasted six decades and for her spare, almost austere style. In this poem we see both of her signature characteristics – the thematic concern with time and the stylistic spareness. Each of the tercets in *The Three Fates* vividly and economically captures a specific scene in the narrative. In the first, we are plunged *in medias res* into an existential crisis. Though the narrative perspective is third person, the narrator is omniscient, which means we are given privileged access to the thoughts and feelings of the protagonist. Dobson uses the narrative device of free indirect discourse to close the gap between observing narrator and suffering character in the second line. The line's syntax could easily have been neatened up to eliminate redundant repetition and tautology: 'To cry out for life everlasting was a mistake'. But, the re-iterative, conversational, more dynamic phrasing suggests a speaking voice, an urgent voice that could be either the character's or narrator's, or, indeed, both:

'It was a mistake, an aberration, to cry out…'

With the simile of the 'cork', the second stanza provides us with a strong, familiar visual image of a man helplessly bobbing in the water. Corks, of course, are small, float and are easily swept away. The language in the rest of the stanza is lean, plain and direct. The focus is on the actions of the man, 'he came', 'put on', 'returned'. There's no time or space here for descriptive details or fancy flourishes.

Time jumps forward, or rather backwards, in the third stanza and the focus shifts from the man's actions to his feelings. The  omniscient narrator can take us into his troubled thoughts. We learn that the man is a poet and that something had made him impossibly sad. In a poem with few adjectives, when they are used they carry greater weight; this man's suffering, we learn, has been 'enormous'.

The emotive language continues into the following stanza which introduces a new character to the story. In combination with 'enormous', agonies' and 'passion', the adverb 'wildly' suggests that there was something perhaps excessive and even reckless in the man's love. This sort of love also implies a relationship with a lover, rather than a child, sibling or parent. Dobson's poem is like a narrative sketch – she provides the skeleton outline of the story, but she leaves interpretive gaps for the reader to fill. Although the poem doesn't tell us explicitly, we infer, for instance, that it is the loss of this woman that has led to the man's suffering, the outpouring of poetry and the tears. In other words, the temporal arrangement of the events implies a causal relationship: this happened after that, therefore this caused that. At a bit more of an interpretive stretch, we might also infer that it is the loss of this beloved woman that leads to the man trying to kill himself. Whether he's lost of her because their relationship has broken down or because she has died, the poem doesn't say. What is clear, though, is that this is a love poem about the terrible anguish of losing love.

What do the series of visual snapshots in the fourth stanza suggest about the woman? Perhaps that she is rather child-like and carefree. Perhaps her actions, 'swinging in the garden', not wearing shoes and being 'straw-hatted' point to a young, free spirit. It's also a scene presumably from summer, a suitable setting for a time of happiness. 'Regressed' is an interesting word to use, because normally the verb is applied to humans and carries more negative than positive connotations. This going backwards, it implies, is both literal and metaphorical, both positive [in that he sees his beloved again] and negative [in that he will lose her again].

The first line of the final tercet is the longest in the poem, thirteen words and fully fourteen syllables. Beginning with a conjunction and featuring four 'ands', the words and their syntax convey how quickly everything is lost and how powerless the man is to do anything about it. The language has regressed to something almost childish, in tune with the man's perspective, and there's a hurrying along, speeding up as we move through the line – three words after the first 'and' then two lots of two and then just one, 'daylight'. And then, we learn, it will begin again 'all over'.

Three lines

What do you make of the arrangement of the poem? Presumably tercets suggested themselves because of the three fates. Tercets also allow the poet to tell the story quickly – in just six sentences. Each stanza is a tercet, so the poem's regular in that sense and there's consistency too in the full-stops that finish each stanza. But, on the other hand, the lineation within the tercets is highly irregular, with very varied lengths of lines, from just two to fourteen words. There's also no metre or rhyme to regulate and order the language, to set if off down definite tracks. Perhaps this form suggests that in its repetition the outline of the story will remain fixedly the same - love, loss, despair, near-death – but that the details along the way may change, both for this man and for lovers everywhere. Hence, like the story of Orpheus and Eurydice, this story is both particular and also universal.

The Three Fates crunched:

DROWNING – CRY – EVERLASTING – CORK – REVERSE – RETURNED – AGONIES – WRITING – TEARS – LOVING – HER – BARE-FOOT – GONE – PAUSE – UNROLLING.

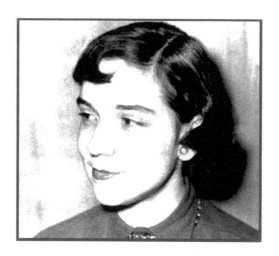

Adrienne Rich, *Amends*

Pointing the way to a non-existent future

American poet, essayist and activist Adrienne Rich [1929-2012] was a hugely influential public intellectual and leading feminist. From the 1960's onwards, Rich wrote from a radically liberal point of view, debunking idealisations of motherhood and wifedom and exploring the complex intertangle of the self with society. The major aim of her writing, according to Wendy Martin & Annalisa Zox-Weaver, was 'to explode the apparatus that had long subordinated women'[9]. Frequently Rich wrote also about her own identity as a white, Jewish and latterly lesbian woman in America and saw 'the struggle of the individual for freedom as coincident with wider struggles for freedom'.[10] Anti-war, committed to issues of civil rights and social justice, Rich's poetry could be angry and tense, or, at times, more gentle and lyrical, as in this poem, *Amends* which comes from her 1995 collection *Dark Fields of the Republic*.

---

[9] *The Cambridge Companion to American Poets*, p.409.

[10] *Oxford Companion to Modern Poetry*, p.515.

The eye of night

The central mysteries of Rich's poem, of course, are what the moonlight symbolises and what it is doing, or, indeed, trying to do. In Classical Literature the moon is always associated with femininity, and, particularly with the Greek goddess Artemis and her Roman incarnation Diana, goddesses connected to hunting, childbirth and the protection of women. Chastity and virginity are especially associated with the moon, but also, because it constantly changes shape, unlike the constant sun, the moon carries connotations of mutability, even of fickleness. Dogs supposedly bark at the moon and werewolves are transformed by the rays of a full moon. Indeed,  moonlight has sometimes been thought to cause madness[11], as in the common phrase 'moon-struck'.

Considering Rich's work as a whole, it seems reasonable to suggest that the moonlight in this poem symbolises a healing, feminine force. What is it doing, or at least trying to do? At first, not that much, just 'picking at' stones, perhaps distractedly, seemingly with little obvious purpose. The next image suggests harmony between the moonlight and the waves as they 'rise', but the light is still passive, rather than active, just lifted by the waves' motion. The following image, however, makes the moonlight more dynamic, with its own agency: Personified as a lover or mother, it is depicted in a gentle, intimate relationship with the land, 'laying its cheek for moments on the sand'. Perhaps this gently tactile image is one of calming and comforting. Picking up the 'mend' in 'Amends', the moonlight becomes a nursing force, explicitly signalled by the animalistic way it 'licks the broken ledge', as if trying to mend it or

---

[11] See, *A Dictionary of Literary Symbols*, pp.129-131.

reduce pain. The mending, curative role - as if it is comforting the landscape and trying to ease its pain – is repeated in the images of moonlight pouring into 'the gash' of a quarry and soaking through 'cracks' of 'trailers'. With the verb 'pours', the first of these images, in particular, suggests great, unstinting efforts to relieve the suffering of a damaged landscape, personified emotively as a body, with a terrible wound, a 'gash'.

By the end of the second quatrain, the moonlight has taken on definite, deliberate agency, moving increasingly quickly over the landscape, although its ultimate destination remains mysterious. Recalling the connection with mutability, it is presented by the poet as a mysterious, protean entity, shapeshifting from human to animal to water to light in a swift series of images. Though the moonlight metamorphises as it travels, one constant is its synaesthetic liquidness – it 'flows', 'pours' and 'soaks'.

Track the moonlight's movements from the start to the end of its journey and it appears to have begun at the shore and then moved inwards, spreading over the land. The location of the stones isn't delineated, but next we see the moonlight on the water, rising and falling with the waves, like a boat. Then it's on the beach before flowing 'up' and presumably over 'the cliffs'. From there it heads into the land until it comes to rest on the 'eyelids of sleepers'. This journey makes the moonlight seem rather like an invading force, coming mysteriously from elsewhere, moving swiftly, silently, almost stealthily, in from the sea.

In contrast to the first two quatrains, the landscape in the second half of the poem is not natural, but man-made – the train tracks, a quarry, a hangar, a trailer park - so the moonlight flows from nature towards civilisation. And why these particular places? Train tracks = lines of transportation; quarries = building materials; crop-dusting plane = agriculture and food supply; trailers = the home. Could the secretive movements of the moonlight be considered threatening? Doesn't the pouring and soaking into the gaps in the landscape seem like a form of invasion? Is it moving in to disable key bits of society's infrastructure and then enter humans through their eyes while we sleep? Okay, I'm getting carried away with the alien invasion fantasy. That might well be a bit far-fetched, but there is something a little bit creepy about this, isn't there, particularly the final image of something that 'dwells' on our eyelids? We'll return to this rather fervid and paranoid line of interpretation a little later on.

Making amends?

Surely the key adjective in the whole poem is 'unavailing'. The adjective indicates that the moonlight's efforts to heal the wounds humans have inflicted on the landscape are, to some extent, ineffective and inadequate, and hence, ultimately, futile. And yet, it keeps on pouring into the wound. The adjective correlates with the conditional phrase the poem ends with, '*as if* to make amends'. The moonlight might be *trying* to make up for something, or the poet may be admitting that this is only a fanciful conceit, only an 'as if' – moonlight, after all, cannot actually heal a landscape – but it isn't actually able to make amends for whatever wrong has been done.

In the whole of Rich's poem, covering sixteen lines, there are only four pieces of punctuation; two colons and three commas. All the punctuation is in the first two stanzas, and most of that in the first. Look more closely at the flow of words in the first stanza: Three words, stop, seven words stop, seven stop again, three words stop. The poem's movement is hesitant, arrested, it moves in fits and starts, an affect further emphasised by the white space in the first line. The comma after 'cliffs', however, is the last piece of punctuation. After that there's no punctuation arresting the flow of the lines, even for a moment, and the poem ends openly, without a full stop. So, as the poem progresses there is a sense of acceleration and of release, or words pouring out. Enjambment ensures lines flow into one another. Though there are stanzas, lines from each stanza are enjambed with the following stanza. From the first word of a poem composed of a long, single sentence, there's a sense that not much could have stopped the onward and outward flow of words across the page, and of moonlight across this landscape.

If we read the moonlight as a maternal, healing force, then its seemingly inevitable, unconstrained spread into the land can only be a beneficial thing. Like the frost in the Romantic poet Samuel Taylor Coleridge's *Frost at Midnight*, it's a natural power, like gravity or magnetism perhaps, one that performs what Coleridge beautifully called a 'secret ministry', healing the earth, or at least trying to, while the humans who have caused the damage are asleep. But, as we've suggested, the moonlight could also be read in a more sinister and ominous light [excuse the lame pun], coming silently at night, entering unbidden and unopposed into homes, into bedrooms, sitting on the eyelids of helplessly unaware sleepers, waiting, perhaps, for them to wake.

Repetition of the phrase 'as it...' crops up in over half the poem's lines and nine times in the last twelve. Syntax is also repeated; almost every time 'as it...' is used a verb, preposition and noun follows. The repetition builds up layers of rhetorical momentum that increases towards the slight sonic twist of 'as if' in the last line. The repetition has also, perhaps, a rather hypnotic effect. Moreover, the phrase contains two complementary meanings – 'in the same way as' and 'at the same time as'. The latter meaning might throw a big spanner into our chronological reading of the moonlight's movement: The moonlight doesn't start at the beach and end on the eyelids; these things are all happening simultaneously. But, actually, surely, both meanings of 'as it...' are in play, and as we read the poem the events do take place in a sequence. Is it more comforting to think of the moonlight as ubiquitous, everywhere at once, or as moving over the land? Or, indeed, more alarming?

In the opening lines of the poem the first light comes from white stars 'exploding'. That's a very violent, destructive verb, especially as the star explodes 'out of the bark', which we must imagine would damage the tree. Compare, the sonically light-footed moonlight which 'picks', 'licks' and 'flicks'. The star is also brighter, 'white' and it has companions, 'then another....' Clearly the poet wishes to establish a contrast between these two sources of illumination. Could the stars, perhaps, be a male force, in contrast to the feminine moon? After all, stars are associated with controlling fate.

I don't know where Adrienne Rich lived or was staying when she wrote *Amends*. To me, it seems possible, however, that she was looking out of a window of a house near the sea, where she saw an apple-tree and beyond it the waves and the night sky. Maybe. Considering her political convictions, I think we can be pretty sure that the work of the moon symbolises the work of women, more hidden, healing and nurturing than the work of men, seeking to repair the damage that has been done. It's an ecological poem, and its open-endedness implies the reparative, healing work needs to continue to be done. Only to an anti-feminist, or ardent climate-change-denier, or a Trump-like figure who is both, might the moonlight's healing work seem like a pernicious threat.

Amends shrunk:

COLD – STAR – EXPLODING – MOONLIGHT – STONES – CHEEK – BROKEN – FLICKS – UNAVAILING – QUARRY – FUSELAGE – PLANE – SOAKS – TREMULOUS – DWELLS – AMENDS

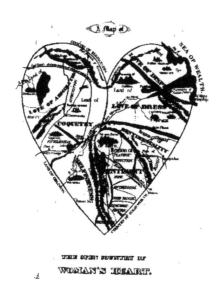

THE OPEN COUNTRY OF
WOMAN'S HEART.

Dennis Scott, *Marrysong*

I've made a small, but significant change to Scott's poem in order to highlight issues of gender. Perhaps give the class the altered one [below] first and ask them to write what they learn about the two characters in this version of the poem and the nature of their relationship. Then read the original and do the same exercise.

She never learned him, quite. Year after year
That territory, without seasons, shifted
under her eye. An hour she could be lost
in the walled anger of his quarried hurt
on turning, see cool water laughing where
the day before there were stones in his voice.
She charted. He made wilderness again.
Roads disappeared. The map was never true.
Wind brought her rain sometimes, tasting of sea -
and suddenly he would change the shape of shores
faultlessly calm. All, all was each day new;

the shadows of his love shortened or grew
like trees seen from an unexpected hill,
new country at each jaunty helpless journey.
So she accepted that geography, constantly strange.
Wondered. Stayed home increasingly to find
her way among the landscapes of his mind.

Not quite a sonnet

Dennis Scott [1939-1991] was a Jamaican actor, playwright, theatre director dancer, actor and poet who has had a major influence on modern Jamaican poetry. Scott often wrote in a Jamaican vernacular, sometimes called 'nation language'. Here, however, the poet uses Standard English to write what looks like a pretty conventional love poem in the great European tradition. From the title, and the fact that the two protagonists remain anonymous, it seems likely that Scott is describing what he believes to be a universal, rather than a local or culturally determined, pattern of miscommunication between the sexes.

Postcolonial critics refer to a process of adopt – adapt – adept to describe an indigenous culture's interaction with a colonial one. Initially the colonised culture is simply forced to accept the values and aesthetics imposed by the colonisers and consequently produces artworks that merely attempt to copy the dominant culture's own. By the end of the process, in contrast, the colonised culture has mastered the alien, rejects its aesthetics and starts to produce its own independent art following different, indigenous values. Scott's poem seems best to fit the second stage, 'adapt', as he utilises the colonisers' language, i.e. Standard English, as well as several other immediately recognisable, conventional poetic techniques. In addition to employing a conceit [extended metaphor] associated particularly with the Metaphysical poets and Shakespeare, for example, the poet lays his love poem out on the page to look like a sonnet, sets it going along a rough pentameter, includes a delayed volta, and ends with a summative couplet in the

Shakespearean sonnet fashion. On the other hand, Scott makes the sonnet form a bit more commodious, adding three extra lines so that it has a lopsided seventeen, and deviates entirely from any set, familiar sonnet rhyme scheme, either Shakespearean or Petrarchan. Reading Scott's poem, we might feel we know the general linguistic terrain, but are less familiar, perhaps, with the local details.

Landscapes of her mind

Through a geographical conceit of comparing a woman's mind to a landscape, Scott's poem expresses the difficulty a man has in reading and understanding his female partner. Throughout the poem the woman's mood and behaviour are presented as being disorientating, unpredictable and changeable as English weather. For instance, the woman's behaviour has no 'seasons', viz no overall larger pattern or design, no seasons via which the man might be able to predict her mental weather. Moreover, while she is imagined as a solid and defined, single landscape, a 'territory', this is described as having 'shifted' each 'year' and as having the capacity to develop 'suddenly' new features, such as an 'unexpected hill'. Her mind is a territory that keeps seeming to contain 'new country' and despite his exploration and attempts to map it remains 'constantly strange'. Only at the end of the poem does the man come to realise that his partner's mind is more complex than he'd conceived; that there isn't one, but multiple landscapes within this woman's capacious mind.

Sometimes these shifts appear to be deliberate, intentionally designed to perplex him, 'she would change the shape of shores'. Though he might forge pathways, just as quickly 'roads disappeared' and so he can easily become 'lost'. Her apparent impenetrability is also conveyed through the concrete metaphors of her 'walled anger' and her pain being 'quarried', imagery that implies she is made of stone.

In a moment and apparently without cause, however, the stoniness can morph mysteriously into 'cool water' and anger transform unexpectedly to laughter. Logically, doggedly, almost comically, the rather hapless man tries to make maps to navigate by. In an immediate apparent countermeasure, the woman, bamboozling his attempts, 'made wilderness again'. His confusion and exasperation are conveyed through repetition, such as in the despairing or perhaps just resigned sounding 'all, all  was each day new'. Without any palpable success, he keeps trying to chart her, treating her like a landscape, navigating her moods, setting out on 'each jaunty' but 'helpless journey'. Until suddenly he has a brainwave.

He stays at home. Rather than setting out on repeated, 'helpless' journeys into her bewildering mental interior, he just stays home. In other words, he stops trying so vigorously to order, predict and understand her behaviour, to chart and map it, and just allows it to happen, discovering as a result, that he can 'increasingly find/ his way among the landscapes of her mind'. Traditionally in a sonnet this turn in the idea or subject is called the volta and happens in the first line of the sestet. Coming across Scott's delayed volta is like finding an expected feature in a landscape, but discovering it further away than you had expected.

What do make of the way the woman's mind and behaviour is compared to a landscape? Would the poem work just as well, if the speaker were a woman describing a man's mind? Is the poet guilty, perhaps, of falling into stereotypes about men and women? Men are from Mars and women from Venus? With his mapping and charting, observing and journeying, the man is presented as logical and rational and rather dogged. She, however, seems mysterious, capricious, perhaps playful, certainly illusive. The features of the landscape – a place without seasons, containing wilderness, with some roads that can disappear, weather including wind and rain sometimes, a shore line, hills trees – makes her seem like an exotic island and a wild, natural, untamed one at that. Think how different the poem would be if Scott had used a sophisticated, urban landscape as his metaphor for the woman's mind.

The man, of course, is the active driving force forging through the terrain, like an explorer or perhaps even a coloniser. In the way the poet presents the man's attempts to 'learn' his partner, there are ironic echoes of the ways colonisers sometimes conceptualised the less developed, 'untamed' cultures they colonised. Except that, importantly, in Scott's poem, there's no conquest involved, no violence or attempts to master or exploit. Indeed, at the end of the poem, the male figure is presented as successfully passive – he 'accepted' and 'stayed home'.

At its heart, the relationship in the poem is based on love, not power. Though, like the sun, it may be hard to see directly – the man sees only love's 'shadows' – and though these shadows change from day to day, 'shortened or grew', the love itself remains fixed and constant.

Reading the poetic landscape

The explorer/ territory metaphor is analogous to our experience of reading this poem. In some regards, the conceptual and linguistic pathways are predictable and navigable; there are 'roads', and we can orientate ourselves within what seems like familiar literary territory – we know where we and the poem are heading. But, on the other hand, there's no rhyme scheme to function as road signs or landmarks: Before the final couplet, only once do we stumble across some end rhymes ['true', 'new', 'grew'] and they spring up seemingly randomly in unexpected places, like flowers in a desert. And only a rather rough and bumpy metre guides us down some admittedly familiar tracks of thought. And just when we think we should have come to the end of our reading journey and arrived at our destination, there's suddenly new linguistic territory ahead, a few extra lines, extending the terrain a little further and taking us in a new direction. In this way, Scott works within, but also against the conventions of the sonnet tradition.

Marrysong mapped:

LEARNED – TERRITORY – LOST – WALLED – LAUGHTER – STONES – CHARTED – MAP – RAIN – SUDDENLY – ALL – LOVE – UNEXPECTED – NEW – ACCEPTED – HOME – MIND.

Elizabeth Barrett Browning, *Sonnet 43*

Barrett Browning's famous sonnet is another poem that lends itself well to an unscrambling exercise. Give the students the poem with just the  first and last lines in the right order and all the others scrambled, as shown below. Their task is to arrange all the lines in the correct order as quickly as they can. But before you or your students attempt the task, it's important to tell them that this is a Petrarchan sonnet, which means there are only four rhymes in the whole fourteen lines. Well, that's not entirely correct; while the opening eight lines follow the ABBA ABBA of the Petrarchan form, the closing six lines, or sestet, follow one version of it, switching to an alternating CDCDCD pattern. One of the major technical challenges of writing a Petrarchan sonnet is the difficulty of finding suitable rhymes without contorting the meaning or making the rhyme words stick out like sore thumbs – hence in Shakespeare's version of the form there's a more capacious seven rhymes. The Petrarchan form more usually used five rhyme words – Barrett Browning demonstrates great technical virtuosity by just using four.

How do I love thee? Let me count the ways.
Smiles, tears, of all my life; and, if God chose,

For the ends of being and ideal grace.
Most quiet need, by sun and candlelight -
In my old griefs, and with my childhood's faith.
I love thee to the depth and breadth and height
I love thee to the level of everyday's
I love thee purely, as they turn from praise;
I love thee with the passion put to use
I love thee freely, as men strive for right, -
I love thee with a love I seemed to lose
My soul can reach, when feeling out of sight
With my lost saints. I love thee with the breath,
I shall but love thee better after death.

Is this poem obviously by a female writer do you think? I'd present it to my class the first time without the poet's name and get them to speculate about the writer's gender. Might throw up some interesting ideas…

A modest disguise

Elizabeth Barrett Browning wrote *Sonnet 43* as a private expression of her love for fellow poet Robert Browning, with whom she had begun a secret courtship. The couple later married, but her wealthy father disowned her as he did not approve of her choice of husband. It was only after they eloped and were married that Elizabeth mentioned she had written a series of sonnets about Robert while they were courting. When he read them, Robert thought them to be the best sonnets written in English since Shakespeare's and encouraged her to publish. However, they were so personal and revealing, having never been intended for anyone other than Elizabeth Barrett Browning herself, that they were published under the title *Sonnets from the Portuguese*, in an attempt to pretend they were obscure translations of another poet, rather than intimate expressions of her own private emotions. Some of the sonnets, such as *Sonnet 29,* are intensely personal and express a love that is passionate and erotic. *Sonnet 43*, in contrast, conveys a more spiritual, devotional and platonic sort of love. Nevertheless, the reader is given unusually intimate access to the poet's private feelings.

Breadth and depth and height

The short opening question immediately creates a sense of a private and intimate conversation, as if the poet is herself repeating a question she has been asked. The language is noticeably very simple. In the first line all the words are common monosyllables and they are employed in a literal way within two short sentences that have straightforward syntax. Such simplicity is testament to the honesty and truth of what the poet is saying; there is no need for her to dress up, inflate, disguise or aggrandise her feelings through metaphor or symbolism. Her language is direct, unvarnished, transparent and trusting.

In the following lines, however, similarly simple words are used in a more complex, figurative manner. Barrett Browning employs a spatial metaphor for the soul, imagining the furthest limits it could possibly  stretch - to its utmost 'depth and breadth and height'. Such is the love she feels that it fills her whole soul, reaches even into unknown dimensions ['feelings out of sight'], to the furthermost extent of her 'being' and it is a love that echoes the very best of herself, 'ideal grace'. And this is a poem very much of the soul; the heart, that traditional symbol of passion and love, does not even get a mention. Instead the poem expresses a spiritual, disembodied, idealized, devoted sort of love. Hence the religious touchstones of 'grace', 'faith', 'saints' and 'God'.

If this version of love seems impossibly idealistic, rarefied and saintly, Barrett Browning brings it closer to the ground in the following lines. Lowering the poem down to a more ordinary pitch, she refers to the everyday and to what we 'need'. The superlative implies, however, that this need is not the mere clamorous cravings of desire, but rather the deepest of spiritual needs. The upright, good, virtuous aspects of this love are then developed. The poet associates her love with the universal progressive fight for justice and praises its resistance to the shallow allurements of ego and vanity.

At this point in the poem we reach the end of the opening eight lines, or octave. As you know, Barrett Browning's sonnet follows the Petrarchan form with a rhyme scheme of ABBA ABBA CDC DCD. The fact that the poet achieves this octave with such elegance and without seeming to break artistic sweat – the words fall naturally on the ear despite having to fit such a tightly controlled pattern - makes it perfectly correlate to the ideal love it expresses. The graceful form of the poem not only fits, but, in itself, embodies its meaning. However, a Petrarchan sonnet has a volta, somewhere around the ninth line, the first of the sestet. Conventionally sonnets have a call and response or question and answer structure, with the sestet [final six lines] responding to the octave. A volta marks a turn in the subject of a sonnet, sometimes signalled with a 'but' or 'however' or similar signposts for a switch in perspective.

However hard you search for the expected volta in *Sonnet 43* you'll not be able to find it. Despite expectations that they must come, no counterarguments to the series of propositions set out in the octave appear. Instead the poem runs straight on and over its expected switch point, continuing to express the same loving sentiments, only now it develops these in new ways. The first line of the sestet, for instance, begins with exactly the same phrase, 'I love thee', as the previous two lines of the octave have done and overall this simple phrase is repeated four times in both halves of the poem. Hence the whole the depth and breadth and height of the sonnet is filled with ideal love.

After the references to grief and faith, Barrett Browning finishes her sonnet with language that is simple, unadorned and poignant:

'I love thee with the breath/ smiles, tears of all my life'

Moreover, such a love, she tells us, will not only transcend death and become immortal, as if that isn't enough! Perfect though it already is, this love will be further refined by death.

The danger with such a restrained and graceful expression of such an elevated, ideal love is that it will feel overly chaste and bloodless; it may seem a love more suitable for angels than for human beings. Though there is a reference to 'passion', this is not the fiery or dangerous passions of erotic or sensual love. Rather it is passion in terms of strong and earnest feelings. Perhaps there is also a little sense of excited agitation in the lines we quoted above, created by a run of unstressed syllables in both lines and the tripartite list of 'breath, smiles, tears'. But on than that small flutter of feeling, the poem is almost impossibly composed. Maybe we need to read some of the other sonnets to find real passion in Barrett Browning's love for Robert. It is surely significant that this poem is the penultimate one in the sequence.

 As readers, we are placed in the position of the beloved. We are addressed directly as 'thee' and this rather archaic, perhaps timeless, pronoun is used in almost every line. How would you feel if someone said all this to you? How might Robert have felt? Delighted? Flattered? Daunted? All of these? Perhaps you might like to write his response, in either letter or verse form:

'Dearest Lizzie my love,
I read your poem and I am moved beyond words can express.
Truly I am an unworthy object of such pure love…'

Or perhaps you could write a parody of the poem, using the same form but bring the noble, elevated tone crashing right down to earth:

'How do I luv ya? let me number the ways:
I luv ya like I luv fish and chips,

As much as minty ice-cream with those chocolatey bits,
I'll luv ya babe, to the end of my days...' etc.

Broadly speaking, historically, sonnets were written most often by men. Frequently they were love poems, often about, and addressed to, women. Women in sonnets tended to be objectified, sometimes even deified as beautiful goddesses. So, the sonnet was a form in which men could show off their wit and write something daringly seductive. Barrett Browning colonises the predominantly male poetic space of the sonnet and demonstrates that she can too handle the form. And that she can do it with just as much deftness, panache and variety as any male writer. In this sense, her sonnets can be read from a feminist perspective. Indeed, Barrett Browning's sonnets equal, or in fact, surpass male artistic achievements in the form [apart from Shakespeare, of course]. In addition, her role as a sonneteer, taking the boss seat in the relationship to express her love for a male 'object' reflects the loosening of rigid concepts of gender and the great advances made by women towards the end of the Victorian age.

Sonnet 43 crunched:

HOW – LOVE – SOUL – IDEAL – EVERY – NEED – FREELY – PURELY – PASSION – FAITH – LOSE – SAINTS – GOD – BETTER.

Edna St. Vincent Millay, *Sonnet 29*

As, hopefully, it did with Barrett Browning's poem, a cloze exercise can help us appreciate some of the key skills involved in composing  a sonnet. A significant difference this time is that Millay follows the Shakespearian version of the form. So, this time, a variation on the cloze task would be to present the sonnet docked of its final summarising couplet. Each member of the class can then attempt a couplet themselves. As suggested with *Rising Five*, these are then to be submitted to their teacher, who reads out a selection, including, ideally one of their own cunning devising, as well as, of course, Millay's original. The class votes for the best couplet. Turning this art into a sport, you could award five points to students whose couplets are chosen. The student with the most points at the end has to compose a new sonnet, using their last line as the first line. And/ or give them a bar of chocolate.

For what it's worth, here's my attempt:
'Pity me not for love that was so pure and true
For one day you'll find someone else pitying you.'

My candle burns at both ends

'Free woman', rebel bohemian, celebrated, flame-haired woman-about-town in New York's Greenwich village, bisexual feminist and pacifist, Edna St. Vincent Millay [1892-1950] led a rich and vibrantly coloured life. A Pulitzer prize winning poet whose sonnets have been compared favourably to Donne's and Shakespeare's, an actor, journalist and playwright, Millay was 'determined to live dangerously in several roles'12. Notorious for her sexual affairs, she wrote with scandalous frankness about sexuality, using traditional forms, such as the sonnet, as vehicles to express her very modern, very progressive ideals.

It will not last the night

Millay's sonnet is constructed as a series of instructions, each beginning with the imperative phrase 'pity me not'. The fact that she has to say 'don't pity me' suggests that this is how she, or perhaps women in general, expect to be treated when they find themselves in her situation. Except that she phrases it 'pity me not', a rhythmical rat-a-tat-tat which kicks off these lines with an emphatic reversal, a trochee, before they ease into the poem's dominant iambic pattern. Millay tells us she doesn't want to be pitied for getting older and losing her beauty, but she dresses these ideas up and projects them onto the sort of romantic and natural figurative imagery we would expect in a Shakespearean sonnet. The first image, for instance, is of dying light, which the poet rather fancifully imagines 'no longer walks the sky'. Something magical, precious and romantic has been lost, the poet  implies, and her present, the 'close of day', connotes aging and perhaps even the approach of death. The poet projects her own fears onto the landscape again in the second image, whereby loss of beauty in the landscape, 'field to thicket' mirrors her fears about her own attractiveness. Perhaps too, there's a more general sense of beauty fading from the speaker's life.

---

12 *Oxford Companion to Modern Poetry.*

The indirect, universalising figurative imagery continues in the third example, in which it's not aging or loss of beauty the poet fears but the mutability of existence, its 'waning' and 'ebbing'. Moreover, in both images the change is for the worse, another decline, this time one in which vitality is lost. The moon, of course, is a conventional symbol in love poetry, associated with romance and the tide is associated with driving energies, powering experience. 'A man's desire', presumably for the poet, is another in this series of losses.

It comes as something as a shock, when, in final line of the octave, Millay introduces a second person pronoun:

'And **you** no longer look with love on me'.

There's a touching emotional nakedness and vulnerability in the direct way this line is phrased. Her pain is entirely open and undistinguished. Millay uses very straightforward vocabulary in a literal, rather than metaphorical way, with simple alliteration emphasising her point about looks and love. Clearly this is the intimate heart of the matter, the reason for the poet feeling so forlorn, the reason, indeed for the poem itself. The entire first half of the sonnet, its opening eight lines, is one long sentence that culminates here with the binary 'you...me'. And the octave ends forcefully like a door being shut, with a full-stop. Sometimes, of course, in a sonnet, poets leave a gap between the octave and sestet. And it must have been tempting for Millay to do so, so that his line would resonate a little longer in the reader's mind. Why didn't she? Maybe because the line does rather invite us to pity her, despite her protestations to the contrary, and for us to truly admire her, she needs to show she can be brave and press on.

Indeed, the first line of the sestet recovers the poem's stoical poise, shifting from the heat of emotions to colder conceptual realms, 'this have I known always'. At this point, the poet switches into philosophical mode, again using natural imagery to conceptualise love. Interestingly, the images present love in diametrically opposite ways. In the first, it is portrayed passively and delicately, as short-lived 'wide blossom' which, in a military metaphor, a powerful exterior force, the 'wind', 'assails'. But in the second image it appears that love is itself the powerfully animating force, described as a 'great tide'. In the first image, the blossom is vulnerable to the assault of the wind, in the second it is love itself which is destructive, wilfully 'strewing fresh wreckage'. Hence Millay illustrates both the powerlessness and the tremendous power love.

Past cure I am, now reason is past care

Who, or what, has been trying to gather the 'wreckage' between the gales? Surely the rational side of the self, the mind. The essential conflict we come to in the summative couplet at the end of Millay's poem is one familiar from Shakespeare's sonnets - that between the cool wisdom of the head and the super-heated passions of the heart. In sonnet 147, for example, Shakespeare imagines love as a disease and his reason as an angry doctor trying desperately to prescribe an antidote. Of course, the doomed heart ignores its physician, with predictably catastrophic consequences. The agonising thing is that, though love and the pains of love can be understood rationally and intellectually, grasped by the 'swift mind'- indeed the swift  mind can even conjure concrete images as analogies to get a grip on love - the foolishly 'slow' heart wilfully ignores these warnings. And always will do so. Like a peculiarly stupid pupil, the heart never seems to learn its lesson. Hence the various disasters of love. Hence the 'wreckage' gathered on the beach after another relationship crashes and burns. Hence falling madly in love with the wrong person or the right person falling out of love with you. Hence the madness and excesses, the delirious intoxications of love, and so on and so forth to time out of sight. And yet, even when reason recognises this whole too too familiar pattern, has 'known' it 'always' and can even compose a decent sonnet about it, darn it, it still seems powerless to prevent the heart hurtling with wild abandon into further similar disasters. And after all the things Millay didn't want to be pitied for, she does want us to pity her for this - for suffering the age old, universal head vs. heart, reason vs. emotion conflict of which her poem is an elegant reformulation.

But, ah, my foes, and oh my friends

The poem, of course, is itself the work of both the head and the heart. Emotion seems to have prompted it, intense feeling certainly animates it. But the arrangement of the words along the tracks of the iambic pentameter and into patterns of imagery and the orchestration of a strict rhyme scheme requires the cool, calculations of the mind. In her own time, Millay was much admired for her technical facility with the sonnet form. Some more recent critics, however, argue that though her sonnets are elegantly constructed, they tend to reprise material covered by other writers and reprise it in a style that looks backwards, imitating what has already become outdated. Sometimes they even suggest that Millay's sonnets are too coolly composed, too brain-directed to really express the true heat of emotion. What do you think?

It gives a lovely light

In my opinion, Millay's best sonnets fill the traditional form with challenging modern ideas expressed in an idiom that mixes the modern with the timeless. Especially powerful and daring are her sonnets contesting conventional roles of men and women in relationships. In this poem she may refuse the solace of pity [though perhaps she protests too much] and therefore appear stronger and more resolute than the archetypally helpless rejected woman. But elegant and lovely though it may be, *Sonnet 29* doesn't quite reach the giddy heights Millay manages elsewhere.

Sonnet 29 crunched:

PITY – CLOSE – BEAUTIES – GOES – WANING – EBBING – DESIRE – YOU – KNOWN – BLOSSOM – TIDE – WRECKAGE – HEART – MIND.

'Poetry is only there to frame the silence. There is silence between each verse and silence at the end.'

ALICE OSWALD

A sonnet of revision activities

1. Reverse millionaire: 10,000 points if students can guess the poem from just one word from it. You can vary the difficulty as much as you like. For example, 'stanched' might be fairly easily identifiable as from Heaney's poem whereas 'poppy' could be more difficult. 1000 points if students can name the poem from a single phrase or image – 'my father crying'. 100 points for a single line. 10 points for recognising the poem from a stanza. Play individually or in teams.

2. Research the poet. Find one sentence about them that you think sheds light on their poem in the anthology. Compare with your classmates. Or find a couple more lines or a stanza by a poet and see if others can recognise the writer from their lines.

3. Write a cento based on one or more of the poems. A cento is a poem constructed from lines from other poems. Difficult, creative, but also fun, perhaps.

4. Read 3 or 4 other poems by one of the poets. Write a pastiche. See if classmates can recognise the poet you're imitating.

5. Write the introduction for a critical guide on the poems aimed at next year's yr. 10 class.

6. Use the poet Glyn Maxwell's typology of poems to arrange the poems into different groups. In his excellent book, *On Poetry*, Maxwell suggests poems have four dominant aspects, which he calls solar, lunar, musical and visual. A solar poem hits home, is immediately striking. A lunar poem, by contrast, is more mysterious and might not give up its meanings so easily. Ideally a lunar poem will haunt your imagination. Written mainly for the ear, a musical poem focuses on the sounds of language,

rather than the meanings. Think of Lewis Carroll's *Jabberwocky*. A visual poem is self-conscious about how it looks to the eye. Concrete poems are the ultimate visual poems. According to Maxwell, the very best poems are strong in each dimension. Try applying this test to each poem. Which ones come out on top?

7. Maxwell also recommends conceptualising the context in which the words of the poem are created or spoken. Which poems would suit being read around a camp fire? Which would be better declaimed from the top of a tall building? Which might you imagine on a stage? Which ones are more like conversation overheard? Which are the easiest and which the most difficult to place?

8. Mr. Maxwell is a fund of interesting ideas. He suggests all poems dramatise a battle between the forces of whiteness and blackness, nothingness and somethingness, sound and silence, life and death. In each poem, what is the dynamic between whiteness and blackness? Which appears to have the upper hand?

9. Still thinking in terms of evaluation, consider the winnowing effect of time. Which of the modern poems do you think might be still read in twenty, a hundred or two hundred years? Why?

10. Give yourself only the first and last line of one of the poems. Without peeking at the original, try to fill in the middle. Easy level: write in prose. Expert level: attempt verse.

11. According to Russian Formalist critics, poetry performs a 'controlled explosion on ordinary language'. What evidence can you find in this selection of controlled linguistic detonations?

12. A famous musician once said that though he wasn't the best at playing all the notes, nobody played the silences better. In Japanese garden water features the sound of a water drop is

designed to make us notice the silence around it. Try reading one of the poems in the light of these comments, focusing on the use of white space, caesuras, punctuation – all the devices that create the silence on which the noise of the poem rests.

13. In *Notes on the Art of Poetry*, Dylan Thomas wrote that 'the best craftsmanship always leaves holes and gaps in the works of the poem so that something that is not in the poem can creep, crawl, flash or thunder in'. Examine a poem in the light of this comment, looking for its holes and gaps. If you discover these, what 'creeps', 'crawls' or 'flashes' in to fill them?

14. Different types of poems conceive the purpose of poetry differently. Broadly speaking Augustan poets of the eighteenth century aimed to impress their readers with the wit of their ideas and the elegance of the expression. In contrast, Romantic poets wished to move their readers' hearts. Characteristically Victorian poets aimed to teach the readers some kind of moral principle or example. Self-involved, avant-garde Modernists weren't overly bothered about finding, never mind pleasing, a general audience. What impact do the CIE anthology poems seek to have? Do they aim to amuse, appeal to the heart, teach us something? Are they like soliloquies – the overheard inner workings of thinking – or more like speeches or mini-plays? Try placing each poem somewhere on the following continuums. Then create a few continuums of your own. As ever, comparison with your classmates will prove illuminating.

Emotional..intellectual
Feelings..ideas
Internal..external
Contemplative...rhetorical
Open...guarded
Declaimed...whispered

Terminology Task

The following is a list of poetry terminology and short definitions of the terms. Unfortunately, cruel, malicious individuals [i.e. us] have scrambled them up. Your task is to unscramble the list, matching each term to the correct definition. Good luck!

Term	Definition
Imagery	Vowel rhyme, e.g. 'bat' and 'lag'
Metre	An implicit comparison in which one thing is said to be another
Rhythm	
Simile	Description in poetry
Metaphor	A conventional metaphor, such as a 'dove' for peace
Symbol	A metrical foot comprising an unstressed followed by a stressed beat
Iambic	
Pentameter	A line with five beats
Enjambment	Description in poetry using metaphor, simile or personification
Caesura	
Dramatic monologue	A repeated pattern of ordered sound
Figurative imagery	An explicit comparison of two things, using 'like' or 'as'
Onomatopoeia	Words, or combinations of words, whose sounds mimic their meaning
Lyric	
Adjective	Words in a line starting with the same letter or sound
Alliteration	
Ballad	A strong break in a line, usually signalled by punctuation
Sonnet	
Assonance	A regular pattern of beats in each line
Sensory imagery	A narrative poem with an alternating four and three beat line
Quatrain	
Diction	A word that describes a noun
Personification	A 14-line poem following several possible rhyme schemes
	When a sentence steps over the end of a line and continues into the next line or stanza
	Description that uses the senses
	A four-line stanza
	Inanimate objects given human characteristics
	A poem written in the voice of a character
	A poem written in the first person, focusing on the emotional experience of the narrator
	A term to describe the vocabulary used in a poem.

GLOSSARY

ALLITERATION – the repetition of consonants at the start of neighbouring words in a line

ANAPAEST - a three beat pattern of syllables, unstress, unstress, stress. E.g. 'on the moon', 'to the coast', 'anapaest'

ANTITHESIS - the use of balanced opposites

APOSTROPHE – a figure of speech addressing a person, object or idea

ASSONANCE – vowel rhyme, e.g. sod and block

BLANK VERSE – unrhymed lines of iambic pentameter

BLAZON – a male lover describing the parts of his beloved

CADENCE – the rise or fall of sounds in a line of poetry

CAESURA – a distinct break in a poetic line, usually marked by punctuation

COMPLAINT – a type of love poem concerned with loss and mourning

CONCEIT – an extended metaphor

CONSONANCE – rhyme based on consonants only, e.g. book and back

COUPLET – a two-line stanza, conventionally rhyming

DACTYL – the reverse pattern to the anapaest; stress, unstress, unstress. E.g. 'Strong as a'

DRAMATIC MONOLOGUE – a poem written in the voice of a distinct character

ELEGY – a poem in mourning for someone dead

END-RHYME – rhyming words at the end of a line

END-STOPPED – the opposite of enjambment; i.e. when the sentence and the poetic line stop at the same point

ENJAMBMENT – where sentences run over the end of lines and stanzas

FIGURATIVE LANGUAGE – language that is not literal, but employs figures of speech, such as metaphor, simile and personification

FEMININE RHYME – a rhyme that ends with an unstressed syllable or unstressed syllables.

FREE VERSE – poetry without metre or a regular, set form

GOTHIC – a style of literature characterised by psychological horror, dark deeds and uncanny events

HEROIC COUPLETS – pairs of rhymed lines in iambic pentameter

HYPERBOLE – extreme exaggeration

IAMBIC – a metrical pattern of a weak followed by a strong stress, ti-TUM, like a heart beat

IMAGERY – the umbrella term for description in poetry. Sensory imagery refers to descriptions that appeal to sight, sound and so forth; figurative imagery refers to the use of devices such as metaphor, simile and personification

JUXTAPOSITION – two things placed together to create a strong contrast

LYRIC – an emotional, personal poem usually with a first-person speaker

MASCULINE RHYME – an end rhyme on a strong syllable

METAPHOR – an implicit comparison in which one thing is said to be another

METAPHYSICAL – a type of poetry characterised by wit and extended metaphors

METRE – the regular pattern organising sound and rhythm in a poem

MOTIF – a repeated image or pattern of language, often carrying thematic significance

OCTET OR OCTAVE – the opening eight lines of a sonnet

ONOMATOPOEIA – bang, crash, wallop

PENTAMETER – a poetic line consisting of five beats

PERSONIFICATION – giving human characteristics to inanimate things

PLOSIVE – a type of alliteration using 'p' and 'b' sounds

QUATRAIN – a four-line stanza

REFRAIN – a line or lines repeated like a chorus

ROMANTIC – a type of poetry characterised by a love of nature, by strong emotion and heightened tone

SESTET – the last six lines in a sonnet

SIMILE – an explicit comparison of two different things

SONNET – a form of poetry with fourteen lines and a variety of possible set rhyme patterns

SPONDEE – two strong stresses together in a line of poetry

STANZA – the technical name for a verse

SYMBOL – something that stands in for something else. Often a concrete representation of an idea

SYNTAX – the word order in a sentence. doesn't Without sense English syntax make. Syntax is crucial to sense: For example, though it uses all the same words, 'the man eats the fish' is not the same as 'the fish eats the man'

TERCET – a three-line stanza

TETRAMETER – a line of poetry consisting of four beats

TROCHEE – the opposite of an iamb: stress, unstress; strong, weak

VILLANELLE – a complex interlocking verse form in which lines are recycled

VOLTA – the 'turn' in a sonnet from the octave to the sestet

Recommended Reading

Bowen et al. The Art of Poetry, vol.1- 20. Peripeteia Press, 2015 -

Brinton, I. Contemporary Poetry. CUP, 2009

Eagleton, T. How to Read a Poem. Wiley & Sons, 2006

Fry, S. The Ode Less Travelled. Arrow, 2007

Hamilton, I. & Noel-Todd, J. Oxford Companion to Modern Poetry, OUP, 2014

Meally, M. & Bowen, N. The Art of Writing English Literature Essays, Peripeteia Press, 2014

Maxwell, G. On Poetry. Oberon Masters, 2012

Padel, R. 52 Ways of Looking at a Poem. Vintage, 2004

Padel, R. The Poem and the Journey. Vintage, 2008

Paulin, T. The Secret Life of Poems. Faber & Faber, 2011

Schmidt, M. Lives of the Poets, Orion, 1998

Wolosky, S. The Art of Poetry: How to Read a Poem. OUP, 2008.

About the author

Head of English and freelance writer, Neil Bowen has a Masters Degree in Literature & Education from Cambridge University and is a member of Ofqual's experts panel for English. He is the author of *The Art of Writing English Essays for GCSE*, co-author of *The Art of Writing English Essays for A-level and Beyond* and of *The Art of Poetry*, volumes 1-20. Neil runs the peripeteia project, bridging the gap between A-level and degree level English courses, www.peripeteia.webs.com and regularly delivers presentations on GCSE and A-level English for The Training Partnership.

With thanks to the eagle-eyes of Izzy & Helena.

CPSIA information can be obtained
at www.ICGtesting.com
Printed in the USA
LVHW030137240320
650927LV00004B/131